THE RIGHT QUESTIONS CAN CHANGE YOUR LIFE.

[signature]

A Gift for YOU!

VIA Technology is honored to support the Women of the Channel Conference.

For All Your Technology Needs

For more information about VIA Technology
please contact Manuel Villa **manuelv@800viatech.com**

WHAT WOULD A WISE WOMAN DO?

Advance Acclaim for
WHAT WOULD A
WISE WOMAN DO?

"Relationships, business, life purpose: it's all here in this book. No matter what your age or your life stage, *What Would a Wise Woman Do* gives insights to support you on your journey."
–**Marlene Chism**, author of *Stop Workplace Drama*

"Every day we make choices—some big, some small. Those choices are the pebbles and stones that form the path of our lives. Laura Atchison's *What Would a Wise Woman Do* shows you how to ask the right questions at every turn to create the path of your dreams."
    –**Melissa Tosetti**, author of *Living The Savvy Life.*

"Laura has taken the art of asking a question to a new level. It is not just about asking questions of yourself or others; it is about asking the *right* questions. She reveals how changing a few words can bring a new perspective to any situation you are facing. Very powerful!"
  –**Dorothy Lazovik**, president of Authentic Leaders Edge Inc.

"Laura helped to clear the sludge from my brain so that my vision became clear. She helped me to recognize that my skills are my own and that I can achieve whatever I set my mind to. She's inspired me to move forward."
    –**Gini Murphy**, president of S.T.A.R. Pilates, Inc.

WHAT WOULD A WISE WOMAN DO?

QUESTIONS TO ASK ALONG THE WAY

LAURA STEWARD ATCHISON

NEW YORK

WHAT WOULD A WISE WOMAN DO?
QUESTIONS TO ASK ALONG THE WAY

© 2013 LAURA STEWARD ATCHISON. All rights reserved.

No part of this publication may be reproduced or transmitted in any form or by any means, mechanical or electronic, including photocopying and recording, or by any information storage and retrieval system, without permission in writing from author or publisher (except by a reviewer, who may quote brief passages and/or show brief video clips in a review).

Disclaimer: The Publisher and the Author make no representations or warranties with respect to the accuracy or completeness of the contents of this work and specifically disclaim all warranties, including without limitation warranties of fitness for a particular purpose. No warranty may be created or extended by sales or promotional materials. The advice and strategies contained herein may not be suitable for every situation. This work is sold with the understanding that the Publisher is not engaged in rendering legal, accounting, or other professional services. If professional assistance is required, the services of a competent professional person should be sought. Neither the Publisher nor the Author shall be liable for damages arising herefrom. The fact that an organization or website is referred to in this work as a citation and/or a potential source of further information does not mean that the Author or the Publisher endorses the information the organization or website may provide or recommendations it may make. Further, readers should be aware that internet websites listed in this work may have changed or disappeared between when this work was written and when it is read.

ISBN 978-1-61448-344-1 paperback
ISBN 978-1-61448-345-8 eBook
Library of Congress Control Number: 2012947876

Morgan James Publishing
The Entrepreneurial Publisher
5 Penn Plaza, 23rd Floor
New York City, New York 10001
(212) 655-5470 office • (516) 908-4496 fax
www.MorganJamesPublishing.com

Author's Photo
J. Scott Kelly
Island Images

Cover Design by:
Rachel Lopez
www.r2cdesign.com

Interior Design by:
Bonnie Bushman
bonnie@caboodlegraphics.com

In an effort to support local communities, raise awareness and funds, Morgan James Publishing donates a percentage of all book sales for the life of each book to Habitat for Humanity Peninsula and Greater Williamsburg.

Get involved today, visit
www.MorganJamesBuilds.com.

DEDICATION

For my mom and dad, without whom I would never have learned that it is good to question, and for creating a safe place to do so. Dad, I am sure God will get a copy of this book to you in Heaven. I wish you were still here to celebrate with us. Mom, thank you for always believing in me. I owe you both more than I can ever express. I am who I am today because of your faith and encouragement.

For my husband, Jerome—who shows me, every day, that dreams are worth waiting for.

For God, who opened my heart to possibility.

Ten percent of all author royalties are donated to non-profits close to my heart including the Michael J. Fox Parkinson's Foundation.

"All achievement, whether in the business, intellectual, or spiritual world, are the result of definitely directed thought..."
–James Allen

"He that seeketh findeth; and to him that knocketh it shall be opened for only by patience, practice and ceaseless importunity can a man enter the Door of the Temple of Knowledge."
– James Allen, *As a Man Thinketh*

TABLE OF CONTENTS

FOREWORD

The question posed by the title of this book invites a lot of discussion. Laura does a better than superb job of exploring that discussion, and providing authentic dialogue and guidance along the way.

The key to knowing exactly what a wise woman would do is knowing the right questions to ask. Laura wants you to master the art of asking the right questions—even if you have not yet done so. She wants you to understand how asking the wrong questions might have kept you from what you are capable of becoming. She wants you to know that no matter where you are, it's not too late to start over in asking the right questions.

So do I.

Why? I fervently believe that in the fool's mind, there are many options, just as there are many disempowering questions.

In the wise woman's mind, there is only one option: to ask the right questions, that guide you to the right answers.

It's only by asking the right questions that a wise woman learns just what she should do.

This book exists to direct you to those right answers by learning to ask better questions. The most extraordinary thing about the right answers is that you already know them: God has given them to you.

Acting on those answers requires you to trust your instincts—something that the wise woman also has mastered.

That is why I ask you to trust your instincts and listen to what God has told you. Learn to ask the right questions, and trust that in doing so you have the right answers.

The answers are in the pages ahead. But mostly, they are in your mind now, awaiting the right questions!

Jay Conrad Levinson
Debary, Florida

Introduction

WHAT AM I ASKING MYSELF?

*"The real voyage of discovery consists not in
seeking new landscapes, but in having new eyes."*
—**Marcel Proust**

I started first grade when I was six years old. Back then, the norm for children was to learn to read once they got to this important milestone. So naturally, I looked forward to my first day.

Unfortunately, it didn't go as I had planned. My mom loves to tell the story about how I left school, walked right out in the middle of the day, and came home. She asked why I was home so early, and I told her it was because they wouldn't teach me how to read.

At the time, I didn't understand why, but I later learned I had been put into the second group instead of the first group. All I wanted was to learn how to read! Since my parents were always reading to me, I knew there was this huge world out there accessible only through the vast universe of books, and I was more than ready to explore this larger world for myself. I had no patience; I was on fire to read!

On that first day of class, rather than figuring out a way to get myself into that other group that was being taught to read right then, my six-year-old self just walked away. I concluded that my teachers likely weren't *ever* going to teach me to read, and as a result I felt angry and powerless. I didn't understand.

My mom, however, did understand—at least that there was something we weren't aware of yet—and as a result, she went to the teacher to talk about why I had walked out of school. Mom knew enough to get to the point and ask her directly why I wasn't going to be taught to read yet. The answer was simple, although not exactly full of merit: I was towards the end of the alphabet so I was in the second group. Due to my eagerness and my mom's persistence, the school agreed to switch me, and I started learning to read the next day.

This experience taught me a powerful lesson about asking questions. That is, Mom knew that by *asking questions, she could change the outcome.* She didn't tell the teachers *what to do.* She asked them *what could be done.* In the process, she showed me that asking the right questions can change the outcome, which in turn can change your life. This has become the lesson of my life, and the one I explore with you in this book.

To this day, Mom says she cannot afford to keep me in books, and she urges me to go to the library. I still use the library, plus Google and the Internet, and anyone I can find who is willing to answer my questions. I have been on a lifetime quest to find the right questions to improve my life—not only in regards to little things, like learning facts about the world—but also in the bigger issues life brings to me.

I am eager to meet anyone who can help me increase my wisdom, and I have made it my mission to formulate and ask the right questions. In that process, I've also made some mistakes, which have led me to greater clarity. In the end, I've found some key questions I'd like to pay forward to you to help you on your own journey.

As you read through the rest of this book, think about what is happening in your life as you explore my process for making choices. I will show you what I was thinking as I made these key choices, what the specific choices were, what happened next, and how I realized when I was asking myself and others the right questions. Then, I will show you how things changed for me.

Finally, I will let you in on the specific questions I initially asked, as well as the new questions I learned to ask along my path to becoming wiser. My hope is that you will gain insight into new ways to ask the right questions, so that you can avoid my pitfalls.

By showing you how to shift your thoughts and questions—even a little bit—you will see opportunities and choices you never dreamed were possible. Journey with me as we explore, *What Would a Wise Woman Do,* in:

Relationships
Business
Times of Personal Crisis
Money Matters
Self-perception
Searching for Faith
Planning Her Future

Before we begin, I'm going to let you in on some preliminary questions you can learn to ask which will help you get the most from this book. We'll explore them in more depth later, but reading over them now will help you as you proceed.

As you read, ask yourself,

- *What am I asking myself around "x"?*

If you can't answer, you are likely on autopilot—which we will discuss in Chapter 1—so stop what you are doing and start applying questions to what you are doing, seeing, and saying. Give yourself permission to ask different questions—or even just to ask questions of yourself and others about what is happening around, to, and within you.

Ask yourself, and others if you do not feel that you are able to see what is going on in your life objectively, *"Am I asking the best question(s) to move me forward and out of where I currently am? Do I know where I want to be?"* Asking others about what they see in our lives can trigger forward movement because it is hard to see the picture when we are in the frame of our lives.

This book aims to help you ask questions along the way that guide you towards being fully engaged with your life—participating in your journey in an authentic way so that you can experience greater joy and fulfillment.

?????
QUESTIONS TO ASK ALONG THE WAY

In regards to overall questions, ask yourself,

- What am I asking myself around "x"?
- Am I asking the best question(s) to move me forward and out of where I currently am?
- Do I know where I want to be?

Chapter 1

HOW DO I KNOW IF I AM ASKING THE RIGHT QUESTIONS?

"You can't solve a problem from the same level of consciousness that created the problem."
—Albert Einstein

THE ALLURE AND DANGER OF AUTOPILOT

I don't know about you, but throughout my life I have found myself on autopilot way too often. It just seems so much easier to get stuff done when things remain consistent.

While I've worked hard to become more conscious and aware about what I am doing and why, I still find it so much easier to slip back into autopilot. That is the lure of autopilot: you only slip into it when you already know the route you need to take to your destination.

The problem, however, is that autopilot doesn't work very well because when you are in this state of cruise control, you are watching but not always thinking. Instead of being present to what you are doing and having conscious thought about your action and place, when you are in autopilot you are simply going through the motions unaware—somewhat like a machine.

When you introduce conscious thought (versus just watching your life happen around and to you), positive change begins to seep into your life. Why do productive changes happen when you are more present? Because when you start thinking in a more aware manner, you often find that what you are doing doesn't make sense or isn't taking you where you need to be anymore. Autopilot doesn't work effectively once you realize the direction you are going isn't the one you want to go in anymore.

Be warned though that when you embrace the conscious realization that your current direction is holding you captive and will never lead you to go where you are meant to be, you are setting the stage for positive and lifelong change.

The reality is that the feeling of ease that comes with being on autopilot is a lie in the long run. It is only a temporary delay of the inevitable pain of growth that will eventually occur. Yes, it is easier to go along with the status quo; but, as time goes by, your ride will become bumpy and, in many cases, you will arrive at your destination not only with extra baggage, but also with a one-hundred dollar baggage fee.

You may begin to realize you are not fulfilled, you are more unhappy than you are happy, you don't know what your purpose is, and you are not satisfied with your life and what you have. *How did I even get here?* might already be running through your mind.

HOW TO KNOW WHEN YOU ARE READY TO CHANGE

How do you know if you are near this point of change? Pay attention to your reactions. When you get closer to consciously engaging in a big change, you will notice a level of discomfort that wasn't there previously. Consider these examples:

- Have you noticed you seem more irritable lately when you get up to go to work, or perhaps when your colleague or boss responds negatively to your ideas? *This may be a sign that you are craving a change.*

- How about when you reach for that last piece of chocolate cake in the refrigerator instead of the leftover grilled chicken? What thoughts are going through your head? Are there any thoughts? Or are you just going for the quick emotional fix—the chocolate cake, my personal favorite—rather than making a choice that gets you to the healthy you? *If it's easy for you to grab the cake without thinking twice, you may not be at the conscious level wherein change is at your doorstep.*

In 2009 when I decided to sell my technology services company, the tipping point came about because I could no longer ignore a feeling in my gut. My autopilot had steered me into a norm of sleepless nights and a lack of heartfelt joy during my days. My temper grew shorter with each passing day.

At first, however, I avoided dealing with these pressing problems, because I knew facing them head on would require radical course corrections I was unwilling to make. Instead, my dissatisfaction with my business remained a giant pink elephant in the room.

For more than a year, friends and peers would point out the problems in my business and my seeming unwillingness to see what was so obvious to them. They would even question my sense of direction. They would ask, "What is going on with you? Where has your joy gone? You used to love this business. If you are unhappy, why don't you make a change? What do you want?" My autopilot would respond with anger that its course was being threatened.

I remember the day when the questions from both inside my head and outside sources became too loud for my autopilot to override. I realized I was angry at myself, not at the questions people were asking me. You see, I had allowed my auto-self to continue to chart a course without my consent.

I had learned to rely on my autopilot to make the necessary corrections to reach my destination, while not realizing that my course should have been characterized by a conscious journey that held my full and constant engagement.

Another problem with autopilot is that it often self corrects without considering the desires of the captain or the detours that open new doors to opportunity along the original charted course. Rather than plotting my own course after feedback, questions from others, or new information that appeared, I had simply allowed autopilot to readjust me—veering me off course and away from the plans I had for myself and my business.

In reality, what I wanted had changed, but I didn't want to acknowledge that truth because I felt doing so would invalidate all of my accomplishments. It felt like I would be admitting failure if I were to radically change course or just simply accept I did not want the business anymore. (I will go into the entire lead-up to selling the company in Chapter 5.)

The ultimate result of the story I just briefly shared about selling my business is this: I love how aware I have become of how much being on autopilot limited my possibilities. I made a commitment to myself to get off autopilot and stay there.

> I NOW THINK ABOUT WHAT I WANT, RATHER THAN MERELY ENGAGING IN A PERVERSE AND UNCONSCIOUS LOYALTY TO THE MOMENTUM OF MY AUTOPILOT.

As a result, rapid-fire questions form in my mind today about how things can change—how I can move and adjust my path in a more positive direction than one that is programmed into my autopilot. I now think about what I want, rather than merely engaging in a perverse and unconscious loyalty to the momentum of my autopilot.

This doesn't mean I always have clarity or know I'm one-hundred percent on track. There are some lingering, "What have I been doing with my life?" moments. I am human after all, and we humans have doubts and fears and seem to enjoy a little bit of self-flagellation. But, as I've learned to challenge the autopilot more, those weaker moments have far less of an impact on my life and happiness.

How Do I Get Off Autopilot?

Steve Jobs was an incredible example of someone who knew the course he wanted to be on. He was determined to let go of everything that did not meet the end result he envisioned. It simply did not matter that the iPad, iPod, iTunes, or iPhone had never been created before. He was determined to avoid life's persistent autopilot and keep making innovative Apple products which no one had seen before. He wanted to wake up the world to what could be.

How can we learn from his example? To get off autopilot, it helps to understand how we manage information and stimuli. Our brains process millions of bits of data each and every moment we are alive. We discard a lot of information without ever having conscious recognition of what the information means. But the data that remains affects the choices we make throughout the day. Those remaining bits of data move into our conscious minds and do their work. They start as mere facts until we begin to process and assign context and meaning to them.

Working from the "Spock Point"

Before adding our emotions and creating context and meaning to the data, we may end up making choices that are merely "clinical." Essentially, we have no emotional involvement in the outcome at this point and are merely coming to conclusions based on the data available at the time.

If you follow *Star Trek* or even have heard of the TV show or movies and their main characters, you might call this the **Spock Point.** This is not a reference to his pointy ears!

For those of you who are not up on TV trivia, Spock comes from the planet Vulcan and is part of the bridge crew of an Earth starship called the Enterprise. His planet long ago suppressed all emotion, and therefore values logic and reason above all else. Emotion does not play any part in the choices Vulcan's make. Pure reasoning, logical deduction, and statistics determine the course of actions they take.

In the series, human emotion as demonstrated by Captain Kirk and the rest of the crew, when added to the data Spock gives, more often wins the day for the crew—versus just the choices available when using only logic. Basically, the crew adds their gut instincts to the data provided by Spock to win the day.

WORKING FROM THE "EXPERIENCE POINT"

Once we gain awareness that more exists beyond just receiving data, we can begin to apply our past experiences, knowledge, learning, and emotions. It is from this point that we make better choices to direct our lives. I call this the **Experience Point.** The Experience Point adds feelings, emotions, and past experiences to facts. This creates a human element that then controls our actions and choices.

The addition of the human element is not bad. On the contrary, the human element can prevent us from harming ourselves or others by making us realize that just because the odds are in our favor for something to work doesn't mean it is the best thing to do. I have seen that making choices only from the Experience Point or the Spock Point can lead to a bumpier path and sometimes one that is a dead end.

"THE REALITY POINT": TYING IT ALL TOGETHER

What if you could learn how to make choices from the Spock Point *and* the Experience Point? What if all the choices you made took into account not only the wisdom you have learned over the course of your life, but also a reanalysis of facts and new knowledge outside your experiences and wisdom—so that options and possibilities beyond what you originally envisioned are present?

This is the Reality Point—that ideal mode of daily thinking that occurs when you are looking at your choices with clarity and consciousness and choosing how to proceed with the best information available. (Chapter 2 will go over this concept in more detail.)

Let's look at an example of how this might work. I like to use the analogy of a basketball game because most people have seen a game or have watched some form of sporting event. When you are watching a basketball game, this is what you see from the Spock Point: a bunch of people in different uniforms running back and forth on a hardwood floor towards raised round hoops with netting at their base.

You see the players using a round orange ball with black stripes and notice they are trying to get the ball into the hoops—and the ones who don't have the ball are trying to stop that from happening. You also notice they get points based on how far away from the hoop they are when they throw the ball and get it in the hoop.

From the Spock Point, you can see there are lots of other rules, but this is the basic idea. You also may be aware of the statistics or odds of getting the ball in the hoop and beating the other team.

From the Experience Point, you may have played basketball or know someone who has—so you begin to add emotion into the equation. Perhaps you have a favorite team who you root for and are willing to overlook mistakes or penalties its members experience.

In the Experience Point, you really only see one team on the court and you assume they are going to win. Or, maybe you have learned that one of the teams never wins against the other team, so you go in with the Spock Point fact that the team will not win this time either and then you ignore it hoping this time will be different.

From the Reality Point, you see all of those things but you decide to watch the game for what it is with no judgments because you know that in sporting events, anything is possible; in fact, sometimes the underdog wins in spite of long odds against them. You enjoy the game as it is played. Even though you have a favorite team, you can recognize a good game from both sides of the field of play.

Die-hard fans much prefer to stay in the Experience Point and cheer their team on to the victory they hope for. Gamblers like to dwell a bit longer in the Spock Point so they can understand the odds but will slip into the Experience Point quite often when they actually place their bets.

Watching a game from the Reality Point is much more fun for me because I actually see all that is happening on the field and can appreciate the skill it takes to do what the athletes do every day. I no longer have favorite teams, but I do have favorite players. They are favorites because they demonstrate skills on and off the field, as well as grace, caring, and excellence.

How do you get to this level where you operate on a deeper plane in the decisions you make—where you are not merely reacting to what happens around you, but you are consciously choosing the best path for yourself? To fully optimize the choices you make, you need to take the first step: *begin questioning your questions and the answers you are getting.*

?????
QUESTIONS TO ASK ALONG THE WAY

In regards to where you are, ask yourself:

- Am I on autopilot?
- Am I responding from the Spock, Experience, or Reality Point?
- Am I ignoring signs I need to change direction?

WISE WOMAN NOTES

Chapter 2

How Do I Question My Questions?

"Knowledge is learning something new every day.
Wisdom is letting go of something every day."
—Zen Proverb

Awareness Moments, Pause Moments, and Questioning Moments

So how do you question your questions? How do you even know that you need to question them? The fact that you are reading this book tells me you are not moving forward in the way you would like, and you cannot figure out why. Awesome! You have already taken the first step: gaining awareness.

You have become aware *there has to be something more.* You aren't sure how to move to the next step in your progress, but at least now you realize there is a next step, and you know you are no longer willing to stay where you are now. *These are your awareness moments.*

After awareness, the second step is to pause. Sounds simple, doesn't it? But sitting in silence, or simply exercising patience, is not always second nature. Many of us are inclined to react—to do something or anything just to not be stagnant. Don't. I have found over and over again that taking action prematurely can be fatal to true progress. Instead of doing something,

10

just stop and take no action until you *know what to do that will move you forward. These are your pause moments.*

So how do you move forward? That is the third step. Rob Lowe, in his book, *Stories I Only Tell My Friends,* says, "All of us on a daily basis have the opportunity to move forward or backward or stay put. Today I know to move forward" (St. Martin's Press, 2011, p. 303).

How do you begin? This is what I call *the questioning moment.* Progress starts by learning to ask yourself these key questions:

- *What questions am I asking myself that got me to this place?*
- *Where did the questions come from?*
- *Do they still serve me?*
- *Are the answers I get moving the dial forward towards my goals, and does my questioning put me outside my comfort zone?*

I have lots of *awareness moments, pause moments, and questioning moments* each week and month. Having even more would be better, because I would then be making more conscious decisions; but sometimes I still react because there doesn't seem to be enough time to run through the options.

I am getting closer to being able to pause first before choosing; but it is okay that I'm not fully there yet. I've begun treasuring each and every one of the moments I do have, because they mean I have reached a new level of understanding about myself and what I am doing.

Awareness moments occur when I see what is really happening in a situation versus what I want/expect to have happen. *Pause moments* need to follow awareness moments and are my favorite because they give me time to breathe and think.

When I experience these, I get a sensation of time standing still. In this suspended, paused moment, I have all the time I need to determine a course of action based on my new awareness. *Questioning moments* often seem to happen simultaneously with *pause moments*—or at least so close to them that they seem simultaneous.

Questioning moments occur when I am faced with needing to run through as many possibilities as I can to narrow down my choices. Sometimes I involve other people in this portion of the process, while other times I might ask myself, *what would (insert a name here) do in this situation?* I always try to pick someone wiser than me when I run that scenario in my head. This is when the question, *What Would a Wise Woman Do?* comes in so wonderfully handy.

You may wonder how I came to this place of being so focused on asking the right questions, and reexamining the ones that got me where I am. A little background may help.

Years ago, I found myself faced with a choice I couldn't avoid making. I was approaching thirty. I had a successful career, my own home, money in the bank to do whatever I wanted with, an incredible mom and dad, and the thinnest body I had known in years. I also had just started dating a wonderful guy.

Sounds perfect, right? Perhaps, but I was about to be faced with a choice I hadn't seen coming: a different man I had dated off and on for a few years suddenly proposed to me. My initial thought was to ask, *why is he proposing to me now, when we aren't even dating?*

It took me a couple of days, but I finally said "yes," and we were married a few months later. The guy I had been dating had recently come off a long relationship so he understood when I told him what I had decided— yet another indication he was a wonderful guy. I should have paid more attention to those signs!

Within four months, the marriage was falling apart. During counseling, I began to realize our marriage was not going to work. We were in different places in our lives, and had different thoughts as to what being married was all about. (I will share more about this in Chapter 4.)

This process taught me that when confronted with the choice of whether or not to marry this man, I did not ask myself the right questions. I learned that instead of asking myself, "Do I want to marry him?" I really needed to ask myself, *"Why do I want to be married?"* Only after answering that question could I ask, *"Do I want to marry him?"*

Once I asked myself the new, critical question, a whole new world of options and answers other than *yes* or *no* presented themselves. I started to look at myself and quickly realized I had wanted to get married because I had not yet checked that box off the mental list I had created that would mean I had "succeeded." Having checked off the marriage box, the only one left would be the "kids" box. Society would then view me as a successful woman, and I would have left a legacy! Right? Not so…

KEY TO THE FUTURE ME

Going back to reassess and ask myself the one question I had previously missed made me rethink my entire life. When I got to the root of it—my desire to achieve something I felt would make me outwardly successful—I had the keys not only to a lot of my past choices, but to a future way of handling things with strength and clarity.

The answer I received brought into question every decision I had ever made. I thought I had known exactly what I wanted from life, and I had a plan for getting what I wanted from early childhood; but upon arriving at this crucial crossroad, I realized I had gone about achieving my dreams all wrong.

John Wooden said, "It's what you learn after you know it all that counts." I used to think I knew it all—that I was the only one with all the answers. I mean, really, who else could advise me better than myself?

I even had a plan for what I wanted to accomplish in my life—be an astronaut—and no one was going to stop me. I did not fully realize the effort involved in becoming one, but that was not going to stop me.

But this outcome of my decision to get married gave me pause. Asking myself why I wanted to get married, and getting the answer I did, made me realize I had a lot to learn about what was driving me and what I believed.

As I studied my past choices, I began to realize a lot of my ideas came from this image I had of a perfect life and a perfect family. What I thought was free will was really the combination of my emotions and beliefs driving me to make choices based on where I felt I *should* be.

WHAT CHOICES ARE YOU MAKING BASED UPON ASKING YOURSELF OUTDATED QUESTIONS?

How does this apply to you? *What choices are you making based upon asking yourself outdated questions? What new questions do you need to ask to get you out of autopilot?*

?????
QUESTIONS TO ASK ALONG THE WAY

In regards to questioning questions, ask yourself:

- What questions am I asking myself that got me to this place?
- Where did the questions come from?
- Do they still serve me?
- Are the answers I get moving the dial forward towards my goals, and does my questioning put me outside my comfort zone?

WISE WOMAN NOTES

Chapter 3

AM I HAPPY WITH MY CHOICES?

"I believe the only thing you can do is be
happy with your choices or change them."
—Lauren Graham

Women are engineered to have many balls in the air and to make decisions quickly while keeping forward momentum. Now men may think it is otherwise, but we as women know what we do on a daily basis. Just think about how we juggle family, work, motherhood, and our households every day.

As women, we are wired to multitask——but this doesn't mean we always make the best long-term choices for ourselves in the process.

I've never been a mom, but I have lots of friends who are, and the one thing they keep telling me is that sometimes you need to pick just one thing and do it. Then you deal with the repercussions if there are any, and maybe make other choices later!

> AS WOMEN, WE ARE WIRED TO MULTITASK—BUT THIS DOESN'T MEAN WE ALWAYS MAKE THE BEST LONG-TERM CHOICES FOR OURSELVES IN THE PROCESS.

If you make a choice and immediately regret your decision, or you avoid making a choice and suffer

16

all sorts of physical problems, this is a sign that the choices you have made are not bringing you true joy.

In the previous chapter, we talked about the three steps to knowing you are not asking the right questions. We said the first step was awareness. Often that awareness is preceded by a physical or emotional response that serves as a warning signal that we are not happy with what is going on in our lives.

We talked about a few sure warning signs in the previous chapter, but it always amazes me how often I ignore the early warning signs that I am not happy with the choices I have made. I often wait until I get the "two-by-four over the head sign!"

BE REALLY, REALLY, REALLY IN LOVE WITH YOUR CHOICES

If you make a choice that you don't really, really, really care about, shift your decision-making around until you find a choice that lights you up. Notice the three "reallys" here. Anyone can care about something, but to really, really, really care you must be "all in" on a choice.

Think about the last time you liked a blouse you saw in a store and you bought it. How many times have you worn the blouse since? Now, think about the last time you bought a piece of clothing you really, really, really liked? Yup, you still wear it, touch it, look at it, and tell people about that item and how you feel when you wear it. Right?

That is why you need to use the "really" litmus test. Three reallys means you are good to go; one means maybe you should wait; and two probably means you need to ask yourself why your choice is causing you to react the way you are. If questioning your two reallys adds a third really then all aboard and full steam ahead!

RECOGNIZING THE WARNING SIGNS

Think about autopilot. In the movies, they often show alarms going off and the pilot having to take the plane off autopilot in order to navigate around a storm or other problem requiring a change in course. If the pilot had been paying attention, he may have noticed weather coming in, a large cloud bank, or even another plane in the air—perhaps even a slight vibration in the plane itself which might have caused him to change course before the audible alarms sounded. The scene would not be so dramatic for the movie if the pilot did things before the alarms went off but in real life those warning signs can smooth your journey.

This is a great illustration about awareness. Our day has so much noise in it. With all that's going on around us—work, family, endless to-do lists, cell phones and texting, advertising pushing us to buy this or do that, and our own agendas for our lives—we can miss the subtle signs that we need to change direction or even just stop for a moment and figure out why we are doing something.

I was taking a class at the School for Practical Philosophy a few years ago, and the coursework one day was around what makes one person wiser than another. I was taking the class via a distance learning program because I love Hugh Jackman. Alright, I know there are other Hugh Jackman fans out there so no laughing! I mean, what is not to love? His smile is infectious, he loves his wife and family, he embraces the roles he takes with passion, he is talented, and he laughs with life!

An interview in *Parade Magazine* mentioned that Jackman had been studying at the school for years, and that he says the school is about "taking duality and finding the underlying unity of things..." I had been searching for wiser people than me for years, so I thought I should see what the school is all about. Jackman always seemed so happy and balanced and grounded. It seemed he was on to something. I have to admit I am grateful my crush on and respect for Hugh Jackman and his talent led me to read that article!

At the end of one of the classes, our teacher challenged us to ask ourselves, "What would a wise woman/man do?" before we made any decisions for the next week. I embraced the challenge immediately as I got a phone call the next day around my business. I was told we had to make some tough financial decisions unless we could get a significant portion of the accounts receivable in within the next payroll cycle.

The issue was not that we had no revenue, but simply that we hadn't collected what was due. We had cash flow issues for the first time in fifteen years.

Prior to that class, I would have become completely angry at the situation and lashed out. Instead, *I stopped and asked myself, "What would someone wiser than me do in this situation?"* I picked up the phone and called a few clients who had the oldest balances and talked to them. I had the money we needed to resolve the immediate need within a week. Rather than waste time pointing fingers or staying angry, I simply did what needed to be done: get money in the door. Then I was able to sit down and decide what would happen next.

What happened next was this: I realized I no longer wanted to deal with those problems. There had been warning signs I'd chosen to ignore for almost a year. Those warning signs included ones from my body wherein I would get sick every time I thought about work.

Other signs—like wanting to stay in bed, cringing whenever my phone rang and I saw certain names on the caller-ID, or even dreading looking at email—happened frequently. There were even smack-on-the-head signs like people I trusted telling me to pay attention to what was going on in the business, and become more active in my business again.

I can tell you this was a humbling experience. I thought I was in control of everything going on, and then realized I had vacated my role and was not in control—and no one else really was either.

I had made plans for my company years before all that happened, and when those plans began to not go the way I expected them to, I chose to stay on autopilot and lie to myself. I told myself that the problems would all go away and get better without my full intervention. I wanted my choices for the business to have been the right ones, but instead those plans had morphed into something that was no longer right for me.

WISE WOMEN PRACTICE SELF-CARE FIRST

I had previously asked myself: "What do I want for me? How do I want my life to look and feel?" I had been asking myself, "What do I want for

> IF I DON'T ASK WHAT I WANT FOR ME FIRST, THEN HOW CAN THERE BE ANYTHING FOR MY EMPLOYEES, COMPANY, AND CLIENTS?

my company and my employees?" But later I learned to ask myself, *"What would a Wise Woman do?"* And I realized that Wise Women take care of themselves first. *If I don't ask what I want for me first, then how can there be anything for my employees, company, and clients?* With those answers, I looked at whether having the company made sense for me anymore. It didn't.

I sold the company eight weeks later, and have not looked back. I began charting a new course that has me enjoying life and doing things I'm passionate about all the time, versus once in a while. I have found that when I'm on the right course, things flow and move me forward quickly. When I'm passionate, it's not a struggle to accomplish goals, and the process of achieving my goals is done with joy even in the challenging moments.

I realized that I had a lot of my identity tied up in my company. I had achieved a great deal of peer, industry, and community respect. Because of those accolades, I felt I had to keep going. When I finally asked myself what I wanted and looked at why it was important to me to keep the business, it dawned on me that all my reasons around keeping the business were because I felt I should.

In my mind, I was a failure if I didn't keep growing the business into the multi-million dollar levels. That notion came from wanting to prove to my dad and others that I could be an amazing success. Part of me wanted to prove something, but I realized I had already done that for myself, and I was ready to move on.

Once I let that old belief go, new opportunities began to come into my life. I met some unbelievable mentors like Bob Burg, Paul Martinelli, Les Brown, Brendon Burchard, and Martha Beck; and I became able to distinguish between what I wanted to do with my life going forward, and what I thought I had to do to please others.

LETTING GO OF PLEASING OTHERS

Do any of you know what it's like to be driven to please others? In the past, I often made the tough decisions even if those decisions did not please others who were involved; but there was always that part of me that felt badly when I had to disappoint someone. I am not yet perfect at making decisions without worrying if they please others, but doing so gets easier with each decision I make. I now understand what was driving me to follow the course I had set long ago.

It's okay to change your mind—or even change course mid-stream—and not just because we are women. Men change their minds all the time, and no one makes comments to them about that!

What is wrong with realizing that something you thought would work just isn't getting you where you wanted to go? To continue on might mean letting your autopilot take you to Antarctica when you really want to go to Hawaii. I've never been to Antarctica, but I know I'd rather be in Hawaii where I can sit on a sandy beach and swim in the warm water.

WISE WOMEN COURSE-CORRECT

It's time for us as women to say to ourselves, "We deserve to have the life we want." I'm not recommending that you leave everything behind and go off in search of yourself like Elizabeth Gilbert did in her powerful book, *Eat Pray Love*. Sometimes that might be your fastest option for getting your life to where you want it to be; but we don't always have that luxury or even that need.

A closer and less dramatic choice involves getting quiet to look at your current life and discover what works, what doesn't work, and what you really want—what your purpose truly is and how to get there. To get quiet, I recommend going someplace where you can be alone. It might even be the bathroom if you have a crazy household, or the beach or a park—or a meditation space if you already have one and can put aside any distractions.

Once there, I like to pull out a journal and write whatever thoughts come to my mind. I love what Gretchen Rubin did in *The Happiness Project*. She stayed in her life, looked at it, and engaged those she loved and cared about in her moves towards being happier. She explored and scientifically tracked how small changes in her attitude and life affected her happiness and the happiness of those around her. She wanted the best life possible, so she decided to look at how she could be happier in her everyday life.

One thing I really connected with was her decision to leave the legal profession behind and follow her passion of writing. She had been a clerk for Justice Sandra Day O'Connor—what I would imagine is a once-in-a-lifetime opportunity wherein she was at the top of her career and could write her own ticket to a next step. Instead, she realized she needed to follow her passion: writing.

That was how I felt when I decided to sell my company. I had no more passion for what I was doing. My joy was no longer there. It was time to move on.

What would your life look like if you could change your mind without guilt? How would it feel if you could make decisions without second-guessing your intuition? What would it feel like if you could quickly go through several different choices and make your decisions based on what you want for your future versus what has happened in the past?

> WHAT WOULD YOUR LIFE LOOK LIKE IF YOU COULD CHANGE YOUR MIND WITHOUT GUILT?

THE FOUR KEY QUESTIONS WISE WOMEN ASK

So far, I've taken you through four questions I learned to ask myself. Those are:

- *What Would a Wise Woman Do?*
- *What Am I Asking Myself?*
- *How Do I Know if I Am Asking the Right Questions?*
- *How Do I Question My Questions?*

Those four questions started me on a path of discovery that opened my eyes and brain to a world of new possibilities that I had only glimpsed previously. If you were to stop reading right here and just begin using those four questions every day for every decision you make, you would be shutting off your autopilot and charting a new course to where you want to go in life, relationships, business, and your faith.

I hope you continue on reading, because in the rest of this book we are going to travel through questions around relationships, money, business, lifestyle, and faith. Feel free to skip around and read a topic that has some special meaning to what you are going through right now, or read the chapters in order. There is no right or wrong way to read the rest of this book. Just read it, enjoy it, and let me know what happens for you.

If you want more questions that guide you to healthy thinking or a community to share your journey with, go to www.WhatWouldAWiseWomanDo.com to get daily questions sent to your email. You'll need to give me your email address so I can connect with you but I promise I will never sell your contact information. Having your information will enable me to respond back to you. You can also visit the forum area where you can connect with a community of other women who are living their lives off autopilot.

So read on!

?????
QUESTIONS TO ASK ALONG THE WAY

In regards to key questions, ask yourself:

- What would a Wise Woman do?
- What am I asking myself?
- How do I know if I am asking the right questions?
- How do I question my questions?

WISE WOMAN NOTES

WISE WOMAN NOTES

Chapter 4

WHAT WOULD A WISE WOMAN DO? IN RELATIONSHIPS

"You are the company you keep."
—Edward and Barbara Steward (my parents)

"WHAT DOES THIS RELATIONSHIP DO FOR ME?" CHOOSING YOUR CIRCLE WISELY

At the end of our lives, what matters most are the relationships we had and the people we impacted. Call this our *emotional legacy*. Most of us want to be remembered as people who made a difference. That is certainly what I want to be remembered for (although I would love to have infinite wealth while I am alive to make an even bigger difference!).

Throughout our lives, we will have many relationships. Some of those relationships will be ones that are not easy for us to be in on a daily basis, while others will be those we don't ever want to end.

My parents always told me, "Choose your friends wisely; you are the company you keep." I believed them then, and I continue to see how powerful that one statement really is—and how it impacts every facet of my life and relationships. I have few people who I consider true friends, but I have a lot of people in my life who are part of my team—helping me grow and learn. People come into and out of my life for different purposes at different points in my life, as I suspect they do in yours.

So how do we choose who to let into our circle of influence? John C. Maxwell, an internationally renowned leadership expert, uses the term "Only Quality People" to define our goal in creating relationships that work for us rather than against us.

Similarly, Randy Gage, another internationally renowned speaker and author I have had the honor to meet along with John Maxwell, says, "If you are the smartest person in your group of friends, find a new group of friends."

They are all saying the same thing: gather people around you who challenge you and encourage you to step outside your comfort zone to become everything you are meant to be. If you are outside your comfort zone, you are off autopilot. Surround yourself with people who are willing to tell you the truth and the reality, versus those who placate you and *yes* you to death.

As women, we tend to surround ourselves with great women friends who hold us up when we are down, celebrate with us when life is great, and hang with us when we are conducting our daily routines. The best part about my girl posse (that's what my husband calls them) is that they are willing to *tell it like it is*. Yes they are supportive; yes they sometimes just agree with me; but most of the time, they kick my butt and make me strive to be all I can!

Stephen King tells a story in his book, *On Writing*, about when he threw away a story he was working on because he thought it wasn't going to amount to anything. At the time, writing about high school girls was not something he felt comfortable with. His wife found the partial manuscript in the trash, read it, and told him she wanted to know what happened next to the lead character in the story (Scribner 2000, p. 52).

Because she challenged him, he finished the story, using her insights into high school girls. That story became *Carrie, one of his most well-known tales to this day.* He kept, and continues to keep, great company who challenges him. This has been one of the things he credits as the keys to his success.

When I started my first company (the one I sold in 2009), people told me I was crazy to leave a comfortable, well-paying corporate job. They said I would not succeed and would be looking for a job in a few months. Rather than listen to them, I listened to my parents' advice and asked myself these questions,

- *Who and what do I need around me to be a success?*
- *What in my life today is not helping me achieve my dream of being a successful business owner?*

The second question inspired a major step forward because it required me to define what I needed to let go of to succeed. I had thought success meant *doing* certain things, but I realized that it also meant *not doing* things.

I quickly began to meet successful entrepreneurs and CEOs who were willing to share tips they wished someone had told them when they first started out. I met accountants, attorneys, finance experts, and business and marketing coaches. They connected me with more people who connected me with more people who would expand my knowledge and abilities. They even connected me with my first clients.

All that happened because I learned to ask the questions that moved me forward.

Something else happened too: certain people seemed to no longer be in my inner circle of friends. I became the company I kept. I didn't always ask the right questions though because sometimes coasting was so much easier. But today, I rarely get to stay coasting, because the people in my life keep asking me the hard questions and I am learning to respond to those questions better. More on this shortly.

Now let's look at the different kinds of relationships in our lives and examine them from a Wise Woman view, learning what we can from each relationship and applying those lessons into other areas of our lives. Chapter 8 will focus on the relationship with ourselves, but the rest of this chapter will talk about the other kinds of relationships that can affect the choices we make.

FAMILY

They say you can't choose your family, but you can choose your friends. I personally would choose my family all over again, but I have several friends who would willingly pick other parents and family rather than the ones they have. Their family relationships were so toxic that they maintain only minimal contact.

I realize I lucked out in the family pool. My parents have always supported me every day of my life, even when they didn't agree one hundred percent with my choices. They pushed me to achieve anything I told them I wanted to do. They had only one condition whenever I wanted to try something new as a child: if I signed up to take lessons, I had to finish them.

It sounds simple enough that I was merely required to finish something, but when you have decided you don't like something because it is too hard or not as much fun as you thought it would be, finishing can be difficult!

Most of the time, I learned I actually liked whatever I was trying, like ice skating, after I got past the hard part of learning whatever was required. This was the gift behind my parents' rule: by not letting me quit, I got through the initial difficult phase and began to experience the joy of mastery.

Sometimes, however, I was quite happy never to repeat an experience— pottery classes being the first example that pops into my mind. I just could not get past the smell of the clay!

Today, I have learned it is okay not to finish some things. In fact, for some things, it's even better never to start when you know it will head you down a path that does not move you forward with your life's purpose.

SHOULD YOU FINISH, OR NOT?

How do you get clear on whether or not you should finish something and find the motivation to stick with it when you find yourself hesitating or stalling? This is when the importance of asking the right questions comes into play.

Whenever I didn't want to finish something, I used to ask myself, "What else can I do besides this? What would be more enjoyable?" Instead, over time I learned to ask,

- *Why don't I want to finish this?*
- *What is stopping me from completing "xyz"?*
- *Will completing "xyz" move me towards my goals?*
- *Why did I start it?*
- *What are my expectations for what will happen when I finish…?*

MANAGING EXPECTATIONS

Expectations are tricky, especially if we aren't clear with the other people involved as to what we expect. Most of the time, failed expectations happen because we never communicated what we wanted.

Rather than complaining about someone not meeting your expectations, try asking yourself, *"Was I clear and realistic with this person and with myself about what I wanted to receive?"* The reason you must ask this question of yourself is because having your expectations met can only happen when you know what those expectations are from the start.

When it comes to family, many of us expect ours to be there for us unconditionally. We often don't understand when they are not. When I considered starting my first company, my parents were not supportive like they usually were, and that got me pretty angry. They could not understand why I would leave a secure job without first having security on the other side. They were fearful I would fail, and they wanted to spare me from failure.

As a result of their fear, they did not give me what I was expecting: unconditional support. I got angry and acted pretty crappy. I actually yelled and asked, "What do you know anyway?" This was not a good way to act considering I was trying to portray that I was ready to run my own company, was it? At the time though, this didn't occur to me.

BE PRESENT TO THE REALITY, AND NOT THE PROGRAMMING

Sometimes the criticism of family can be enough to bump us off course. When my own family asked me to think about staying where I was working, besides reacting, I also took their words to heart. I questioned my decision to leave, and almost backed out of doing so. If I had backed off, I know my life would not be what it is today.

I would have stayed at that job and been increasingly unhappy, probably gotten even sicker than I had been from the Lyme Disease I would later acquire, and would never have written this book. (We'll discuss some of the health issues I have been through and had to watch others go through in Chapter 6.)

It's also possible I would still have started my own business, but would have taken a few more years to do so…and there would have been a lot more gray hairs to be covered by hair color!

How do we wade through our initial fears and reactions from others, and make wise decisions for ourselves? I have found doing so takes an approach that requires listening with many different senses, and asking the right questions to get to the heart of the matter.

Here's what I did: since I had a deadline in which I could accept the employment separation package being offered to everyone in our division, I realized I needed to make a decision and make the best one I could at the time. Rather than stay in fear, I asked a friend to help.

She asked me, "What are your parents afraid of, and should you be afraid of it too?" I realized they were afraid I would end up broke if I failed, because they had lived through the Depression.

That was definitely a concern, so I asked myself, "Do I have a monetary buffer, and how long will that last?" Since I was planning to take a separation package from my corporate position, I knew I had six months' pay and a year's medical benefits to fill the gap in addition to my savings. That allowed me to check off that fear and worry.

In other words, I was able to detach my own situation from their fear, since their concerns were based upon a situation that didn't apply to me.

I also knew I had marketable skills that were highly in demand at the time—information technology—and that I could find a job in six months or a year if my business did not pan out. The economy was different back in 1994. It was before the dotcom bust when anyone with a degree and experience in technology pretty much was guaranteed a job somewhere. Times have changed since then, and perhaps I would not have taken the leap if 1994 was 2012. I'd like to believe I would have though.

By questioning why my parents were reacting the way they were rather than reacting to their fears, I was able to get a better plan for myself and step forward more confidently. As a result, when confronted with a reaction from others about choices I am making I now ask myself, *"Does this person's reaction have anything to do with me and this situation, or is it about his or her history and fears?"*

While most families want their family members to succeed, you may be part of a family that is not supportive. That's okay; you can apply this same wisdom to anyone in your inner circle who may question you.

Whether your family, friends, peers or significant others are supportive of you or not, remember to ask yourself where their questioning is coming from, why their concerns are affecting you the way they are, and whether or not you need to do anything with their statements and questions.

Sometimes, you merely need to let feedback from family slide over you like Teflon. Other times you need to start asking yourself why others' reactions get you mad and make you want to stop what you are doing— or why you want to do what they are saying. Once you take away the emotional charge in the relationship, you turn off the autopilot and are *present to the reality and not the programming.*

CHILDREN

I've never had children of my own. Even with two marriages, God never blessed or cursed me, depending on which parents I ask! I used to feel that I had to have children, otherwise I would have no legacy to leave, no one to follow after me. It has taken all of my life to realize where that belief came from, and I still struggle with it.

Even in the Bible, children are stressed as the most important product from a marriage. You get married and have kids. Otherwise, why get married? So I must want kids, right? Let's explore how I came to where I am today on this subject.

When I got engaged for the first time, I could not stop obsessing over the question, "How soon will we have children?" I ended up breaking off the engagement because he said he wanted kids, but I learned he had plans to have a vasectomy so it would never happen during our marriage.

I am grateful to the parish priest we went to for pre-marital counseling who raised the question that provided these answers from him. I realized if he had been willing to lie to me about that, there were probably other things he might have been lying about. Plus, I thought I wanted kids.

In my current marriage, I kept asking myself essentially that same question, "When will we have children?" After trying unsuccessfully to get pregnant, I went the medical route, and was told there was no visible reason why I could not have children.

It wasn't until I started talking to some friends who did in-vitro fertilization or adopted that I began to question whether I really even wanted to have kids. A dear friend of mine had twin boys at fifty and became even more radiant and at peace after their birth than she was prior. With a role model like her, you could see why I was thinking having kids made sense in my life.

Sounds amazing that I had such a shift, doesn't it? Prior to that point, I had only asked myself, "When will I have children of my own?" Now I realized I needed to I ask myself,

- *Do I want kids? Why or why not?*

The first question takes for granted that children will happen, while the last ones open up a completely different option.

As girls, we are raised to be wives, mothers, and nowadays often business people as well. In some countries and religions, we are not given a choice as to what we are going to be or do with our lives. It is programmed into us by church, movies, books, media, and our friends and family around us who are in marriages and are mothers that the natural progression is to get married and have children—putting aside whatever career or journey we were on prior to getting married.

I felt and sometimes still feel like a failure for a brief moment when someone asks me if I have any children, and I have to answer by saying, "No, I have a dog though!" Heaven help me if they ask my mom if she has any grandchildren when I am around! I sometimes just cannot let go of that awful feeling in the pit of my stomach—you know the one that almost feels like your heart is breaking and your stomach is in your mouth? I sometimes can't get over the thought that I disappointed her because I did not give her anything other than a granddog.

So why do I sometimes still feel like a failure? Somewhere along my journey to adulthood, I got on autopilot for "what makes a woman complete." I bought into the story that you must have kids. Intellectually, I now know that isn't true, but somewhere deep inside there is still a little girl who wants to have babies. Much of that conditioning is due to the autopilot I mentioned. Do you see how hard it sometimes can be to shake autopilot, even when you are aware of it?

Perhaps some of the conditioning also is because my brother died when I was young. (More on this in Chapter 9.) I remember feeling I needed to give my parents another child to love. Regardless, despite having learned to be okay with my situation, I still experience twinges of emotion regarding this subject.

The reality is, I don't have children. It is not through lack of trying over my married years, but because I never got pregnant. We decided not to adopt or pursue fertility methods, so we do not have children. When I questioned myself as to the "why no children" question, and my husband

and I discussed it, we decided it was not meant to be if we had to work that hard at it. And therein is the lesson I want to impart to you. It is totally okay to want kids, and it is totally okay not to want kids, and it is totally okay to want kids and never have them.

What I hope you take from this section is that you need to take yourself off autopilot, make a conscious choice, and be okay with that choice. Having a baby is not something to take lightly. If you have the ability to choose for yourself, isn't it better to make having a child be your conscious choice and not one resulting from societal norms or childhood programming?

Once I asked myself if I wanted kids, I created an opening to be okay not having them. I couldn't and still can't completely answer this for myself. I believe if you cannot answer a question with a definitive *yes* or *no* then you should wait until you are clear.

Patience is not one of my strong suits, but I am learning when I move forward, even when I have no strong opinion one way or another, I often end up unhappy. Sometimes I surprise myself and enjoy something even when I wasn't sure about doing it; but most times, saying *yes* when I am not certain means I will be reevaluating the decision later. Here are the questions that float around my head when I ask myself if I want kids and why:

- *Do I want them because I like being around them?*
- *Do I just want to have someone to take care of me when I get older?*
- *What does the warm feeling inside mean that I get when I hold babies?*

I like kids. I love holding babies, and I love watching them play and learn and grow. But I don't seem to have that gene that makes me have passion for raising children.

All my friends with kids tells me that the moment you hold your own baby in your arms magical things happen and you wonder why you didn't have children sooner. For now, I am quite happy to send them home to their parents after my turn is over. What I love most about children is teaching them new things; but I am content, for now, doing this for short durations.

The Beauty in Asking *Why?*

I don't know about you, but one of the things I reflect on about kids is the never-ending questions they always seem to have at hand. If you are the parent of a five-year-old, you probably feel that "why" is the worst word in any language.

I drove my parents crazy from an early age because I always wanted to know why something was the way it was. "Why do we have to do it that way? Why is the sky blue? Why is it called a chair? Why can't I do that?" You get the drift.

When they didn't have the answers, they made me research them, and then tell what I had found. This ended up being great training for me, and developed my lifelong love of reading, research, learning, and questioning. I still ask my mom lots of questions, but my husband now bears the brunt of me asking him *why* all the time!

Thankfully, he often has great answers that make total sense. I may still want to figure out a different way of doing something, but at least he gives me good answers to work from!

One reason I would love to have kids is to remind me to question things, and to have fun in all that I do. I love that kids question so much, and I love that I get to send them home when they get cranky.

Why is a kid's questioning so important? Questioning opens you up to new possibilities. Good questions move you from your comfort zone into a new perspective. From there, you can chart a new path, redesign your business, create a new product, increase your bottom line, improve your marriage, or even improve your mood.

Asking *why* of yourself, others, and situations, shifts your brain into new pathways it would not typically go down in response to something or someone. I am not advocating acting like a five-year-old, but I do suggest you have an open mind like a five-year-old does (unless it is about brussel sprouts, and then good luck with any five-year-old, or me!). Anytime you find yourself responding on autopilot or feeling like you keep getting the same result that you don't want, ask yourself a few questions:

- *Why am I doing this?*
- *Why do I want to do this?*
- *What can I do to change the outcome?*
- *Where can I get an answer?*

Yes, "why questions" often lead to what, how, when, and where questions.

Keep questioning *why* like a five-year-old, to shift your perspective and create something wonderful—or perhaps see where something might not be so wonderful. For me, I still need to keep asking myself why I think I want children, because I know I have not gotten to the root of that question yet; but for those of you who have kids, congrats and I'd love to hear why you wanted them. You can go to www.WhatWouldAWiseWomanDo.com and send me an email. Maybe you can help me. Or perhaps this is not really a logical thing to be analyzed. What are your thoughts?

MY CHILDREN HAVE FOUR PAWS: PETS AS CHILDREN

"Mom, can we have a dog?" My brother and I asked my parents that question year after year and always got a clear *no*. That is, until we asked one Sunday when I was around seven years old. The difference? I changed the question to, "Can we get a dog *today?*"

They said we could, but only if we could find a place open to buy one. Back in the sixties, stores were not open on Sundays. I think they figured there was no way we could find a pet store open, so there was an easy way out of our request. My brother didn't even want to try to find a solution, but I did!

I grabbed the phone book and started calling around to the pet stores in the area (yes, I used a phone book since the Internet was not around back then). Puppy Palace, in Yonkers, New York, where we lived at the time, was the only place that had an employee answer the phone. Success was close!

I convinced the guy who was working to let us come by within the hour and see the dogs. They weren't even open, but he was there anyway. It doesn't matter why. All that mattered was he was there and I convinced him (remember I was seven years old) to let us come in.

We arrived within the hour with two shocked parents and an awed brother. Here is my favorite part. The guy walked up to my mother and said it had been nice talking to her on the phone. She pointed at me and said, "You spoke to my daughter, not me." His surprised look was pretty funny to see!

My mom asked him why he opened for us and he said, "Because your daughter convinced me that it was worth it."

That day, we picked out our first dog, Patches. It was love at first sight for my brother when the puppy walked up and peed on his sister!

Changing the question that wonderful Sunday created an opening for a *yes* versus the typical *no* we had gotten for years. Sometimes the change comes from persistence and "wearing the other person down" in a positive way. Sometimes it comes by showing someone how committed you are to the desired outcome. Other times, change is manifested through the way you word a question or look at a problem.

Going from, "Can we have a dog?" to, "Can we get a dog today?" worked and got us, after persistent phone calls and lots of questions to the shopkeeper, a wonderful sixteen-year family member.

Pets teach us so much more than we realize, especially around asking questions. *Why*, you ask? (See, the power of asking questions is already working!) Pets cannot speak to us like humans, so we need to use deductive questioning to figure out what their needs are. Similar to babies, pets teach us their non-verbal cues like, "I'm hungry; I want to go out;" or, "Play with me and scratch my ears."

Learning to ask questions, one at a time, and looking at the answers you are getting is one key in finding deeper answers to life's questions. Rapid fire questions with no pauses for new input will only give you the answers you want, not the answers you need—because you will not be giving yourself time to evaluate and assess the answers and match them to the reality (versus the perception) of the situation.

Since Patches, I have had two other dogs: Max, and now Frankie. They are my children, and I have stopped making excuses for how I treat them. It truly is a dog's life in my house! If my husband's cat, Smoky, had not passed away shortly after we got married, we would have cats in the family as well.

If you have added a pet to your family, whether you are single or have a large family, take the great opportunity to ask a lot of questions of yourself and others in your ownership process. We'll go into some of those in a few moments.

Before I got my first Boston Terrier, Max, I was newly divorced and was visiting Brooklyn, New York, with my friend for a one-day bridal fitting for her wedding gown. At the end of the day, we walked past this pet store, and there was this perfect little black and white bundle in the window. I had wanted a dog for years, but my previous husband had refused because we both worked long hours. He did not think it was fair to a dog to leave it alone at home while we were at work.

Michelle knew I wanted one, so in we went—and I proceeded to fall in love with this puppy. I had never heard of Boston Terriers before, but I adored this puppy! We hung out there for close to an hour, killing time until her dress was ready to take home. All I kept saying was, "I can't get a dog," over and over and over again.

Finally, Michelle turned to me and said, "Why not? You are divorced

JUST BUY THE DOG!

now, you started your own company, and you work from home. Plus, you set your own hours. Just buy the dog!" Well she actually used a couple of choice words in the middle of that statement, but I think you get the point.

Talk about a kick in the head and an instantaneous "off autopilot" moment! I asked myself, *why not?* and realized she was right. All the reasons were from my past—and from other people's ideas of what would work for me—versus what I wanted for myself.

We walked out of the store with Max, and he and I had ten wonderful years together. All my clients and staff knew him because he came to the office and often went on client calls with me. If Michelle had not asked me, *"Why not?"* I would have walked out of that store without a dog, and missed out on starting my own family.

Pets are our children for those of us with no human children. Why can't pets be children? We love them, care for them, watch them grow up, and teach them right from wrong. The big difference with children is that kids leave the nest, while pets do not—hopefully anyway!

If you already have a pet, you've probably asked yourself plenty of questions before choosing your pet, or perhaps the pet chose you and just showed up on your doorstep one day. Or maybe you became an instant family after you got married and joined houses with a pet owner. If you are considering getting a pet for the first time, replacing a recently deceased one, or maybe adding to your growing pet family, try asking yourself a few questions to make the final choice the best one possible. Ask yourself:

- *Why do I want a pet?*
- *Am I prepared to make the time commitment involved with training, or am I better off getting an older pet that has already been trained?*
- *What kind of pet do I want—one I have to walk, or one that goes in a litter box or a cage?*
- *Am I willing to take on the responsibility for another being that relies on me completely for its entire lifespan?*

Yup, that was a biggie for me, and I found I just needed to take it day by day because if I thought of forever, I would never move forward with any choice I made. Pets love us, need us, and comfort us no matter how they are feeling. They just want to give and receive love all the time. And of course they play a lot. I think they are the perfect addition to any family as long as you are committed to their care.

The animal shelters are filled with animals left there because they were received as gifts, or they required too much care, or their owners were older or didn't or couldn't take care of them anymore. Consider adopting a pet at your local shelter. Older pets make great family members too!

FRIENDS

I always thoughts friends were for life. We lived on a dead-end street when I was growing up, and there were kids everywhere. We all hung out together, and thought those friendships would be forever. Then, families started moving away, and the friendships grew apart. I only have one friend from grammar school who I am still in touch with on a deeper level than through random Facebook posts. Most of my close friends today are adult friends I met since I started working.

Friends are important to me. When I am feeling stressed out, my husband will look at me and say, "Go get your girl on." What he means is, *call a couple of your female friends and run up the phone bill. Go hang out with them and do whatever it is you women do all hours of the night.* Thank you, AT&T, for unlimited calling plans! There is nothing better for me than talking something out with my girlfriends. I process so much better out loud than I do internally.

Men seem to process differently. Me—I need to talk my problems out, and then the answer just comes. Sometimes I have to talk things out a couple of times with a few different people, each of whom has a different perspective—even though ultimately the knowledge of which is the best answer comes from inside myself.

Do you have friends you can speak openly to—who listen and give advice, or just allow you to come to your own answers? Or do you have friends who tell you what to do and not do? Do you have friends who challenge you to move forward, or friends who just encourage you to stay where you are because it is safer and easier for them?

My friend Pam tells it like it is. She is direct and clear about what she needs from her friends and family, and she is a great listener. She rarely stays stuck on one path, and probably is the friend I have who is least on autopilot. Her patience for people who stay stuck—when there are lots of options to get unstuck—is pretty short, as is mine, which is why we get along so well. I admire that in her.

On the subject of patience, I still get a little annoyed at myself for being impatient with people who cannot seem to move forward; but then I ask myself why that bothers me so much. I typically find there is an area of my life I am stuck in, and watching the other person stay stuck draws attention to my own "stuckness." Once that awareness comes, I can find a way to move forward.

As we discussed in the section about family, it's important to have clear expectations of friends, and communicate those expectations. I know I am not always clear about my expectations, and have suffered disappointment and frustration as a result. I've gotten better at being clear though.

> ...IT'S IMPORTANT TO HAVE CLEAR EXPECTATIONS OF FRIENDS, AND COMMUNICATE THOSE EXPECTATIONS.

Now I stop and ask myself, *"Was I clear about what I wanted or needed, or did I expect the other person to just know what I wanted (otherwise known as 'please read my mind')?"* If the answer is *no*, then I need to apologize to the other person for getting mad or frustrated. How was he or she supposed to know?

As women, we are taught to be the mediators—the people in the relationships who compromise to smooth things over and keep everything "nicey, nice." As I've gotten more comfortable in my own skin and learned what truly makes me smile on the inside, I realized that is all #%&! (you can infer the word).

Yes, someone has to be a mediator, and perhaps even compromise— and women have brains which are naturally wired to see lots of different options—but that does not mean we have to give in, give up, or give away our wants, needs, and joys.

If you want to move forward and achieve all you are meant to achieve and want to achieve, you need friends like Pam around you. Look at your circle of friends and ask yourself:

- *Do they challenge me to move forward or to stay where I am?*
- *Do they tell me the truth or the truth I want to hear?*
- *Are they successful at what they have chosen to do, or do they make excuses for why they fail?*
- *Am I the smartest person in my circle of friends?*
- *Do I dread getting emails or phone calls or running into these friends unexpectedly?*
- *How do I feel after I spend time with friend "x"?*
- *Are the friendships two-way relationships? This means, are they/am I always taking or giving? If I am always taking, then it is time for me to ask myself why and stop doing that.*

Friendships need to be two-way relationships. If they are one-way relationships, they will break quickly. Think of that friend who always calls you to vent about her latest drama. What about the friend who borrows money all the time? How about that friend who calls all the time to say how she just cannot find a job, but never seems to work at getting a job? After a while, these types of friendships get pretty tiring and draining.

If you are at that point with some friends, talk to them about where you are in your relationship with them. Maybe they just need someone to tell them to "stop it." Marlene Chism, bestselling author and expert on stopping drama in life and business (www.StopYourDrama.com) says that most drama occurs because people don't just stop it. They keep feeding off the energy from their past instead of just stopping the focus on past events and living in the now. If we would only release our resistance to moving forward, she teaches, the drama in our lives would be reduced significantly.

So maybe no one has told your friends or you to look at why old issues keep getting rehashed rather than saying, "Okay. Done with that. Moving on."

Decide after you talk with such friends if they should remain in your inner circle or move to the outer rim—or even off the friend list altogether. You don't even need to tell them they are off. It can be like Facebook: they don't get a notice if you defriend them.

The difference here is that it can be awkward when you don't answer their phone calls, or you cross to the other side of the street when you see them. I prefer to be more honest. Granted, sometimes that can be tricky, but it is *your* life, not theirs. If being around energy-draining friends is holding you back, you need to move on.

Sometimes friendships drift away naturally. Think about how many friends you still have from childhood, college, your first job, or the last neighborhood you lived in. For most people, it is not many. Other times, you need to make conscious choices about whether a friendship is toxic and smothering, or uplifting and supportive.

Remember that it is your choice who you are friends with—versus family who you are born into relationship with. Make the friendships the best they can be for you and them. If you don't have any friends, I encourage you to ask yourself, *why* and go find people to be part of your inner circle. Everyone needs a friend.

Spouse/Significant Others

As I mentioned in an earlier chapter, when my first husband proposed to me, I had asked myself, "Do I want to marry him?" This was a really great question, or so I thought, since we were not dating when he proposed to me. We had broken up and I was dating other people. I only had two questions in my head, "Why is he proposing to me now?" and, "Do I want to marry him?" He had a great answer for the first question so I said yes, and we divorced within two years. Our marriage really had ended after only four months.

During marriage counseling—in a last-ditch attempt to avoid divorce—I realized if I had asked myself,

• *Why do I want to get married?*

before I asked myself, "Do I want to marry *him*?" the result would have been different. The response to *why do I want to be married* was an eye-opening one.

I realized I wanted to be married because marriage was the next logical step in my path. I had a successful job, my own home, the respect of my peers, and what seemed like a bright future. What I didn't yet have was a husband. I thought I needed to check off that box to complete the success picture. (And I still am working on clearing that same box I have about having children, as you saw a few pages ago.)

I bring this up again to stress how freeing the moment was for me when I realized that many of the decisions I made about marriage were related to my past, and not to the present or future I wished to have. All my preconceived notions of what success meant to me dropped away and created an opening for me to start my own business, and date only who I really wanted to date versus someone I thought I should date. This meant I could be okay being single and happy.

I dated off and on after the divorce, but I always asked myself the "why" question whenever I started getting serious. For this reason, I remained single until I met my current husband. He proposed after three months. At that time, the answer to my "why get married" question changed to, "I want to get married because I want to spend the rest of my life with this man. I love him and want him in my life every day," versus, "I want to be married to be married." Very different answer. Very different marriage.

Are you asking yourself *why* enough, *or are you just letting your existing ideas shape your future?* Stop right now and think about a project you are working on at work or home. Ask yourself:

- *Why am I doing what I am doing, and does it move me forward towards my goals I have for my future?*

Then ask yourself,

- *Why do I have these goals? Are they mine or someone else's for me?*

If they are someone else's goals or dreams, decide what you really want for your life, and craft new goals.

I have a number of friends and family members who have very long marriages—fifty years or more—and some who really just seem to need to get a divorce. What's the difference? When I ask the long-time married people why their marriage has lasted, they almost always say the same thing, "We talk to each other and ask each other questions to keep learning about each other."

The ones who are close to divorce, on the other hand, have stopped talking to each other long ago about what moves them and what they need. They are like two ships passing in the night: the lights are on but they really are not interested in seeing what is happening to make the lights glow.

Remember your first date with the person you are currently with? (If you are single and not dating, we will get to that in a moment.) Didn't you ask a lot of questions about each other? Why does that have to stop just because you have been together for a while?

I don't mean the where-do-you-want-to-eat-tonight or do-you-want-to-go-to-the-movies types of questions, although those are useful ones too. I mean are you asking the what-lights-you-up and the how-was-your-day questions, wherein you actually sit down and give your one-hundred percent undivided attention to the answers?

If you dread sitting down and talking, consider a marriage counselor or pastor to help with opening the lines of communication. If that still does not work, and you honestly answered questions as to why it doesn't, perhaps it is time to ask yourself some harder questions. I don't advocate divorce, but I believe sometimes divorce is the right answer.

I ended up getting my first marriage annulled ten years after my divorce. Father Mike, my parish priest, told me that God does not want us to be unhappy or in a relationship that does not feed our souls. He said I had tried to make it work, but it was an impossible situation. That is why it was so important to me to be clear about what I wanted next, and be in alignment with a larger purpose and faith.

SINGLE AND LOVING IT? OR JUST SAYING YOU ARE?

On to all the single girls—and that is not a reference to Beyoncé. (That song gets me dancing though!) If you are not dating, is it because you have not met anyone you want to date, or are you stopping yourself from meeting your soul mate because of a bad experience in the past? I think it is totally okay not to be dating, but only if that is what you truly want to do, and you are not complaining to your friends that you never seem to go out on dates.

If you are whining to your friends that you never seem to go out on dates, but you are not doing anything to meet someone to go on a date with, then there is a disconnect between what you are saying and what you are doing. That is a signal to pause and ask yourself *why*.

Embrace being single if that is your path. Embrace it, revel in it, and have fun with it.

If you don't want to be single, I have an assignment for you. Write a letter to your best friend, God, the universe if you are more comfortable with that concept than God, or your therapist—I don't care who, as you will not actually be mailing it. In the letter, describe your life with the person you want to be with.

Describe the feeling you'd have as if you were *already* in that relationship. Be detailed, but remain focused on the feelings and images that come to mind when you get quiet with yourself, and write down only those thoughts.

Don't write from what you think you want or what you feel the relationship should be. Describe your home, the friends in your life, children if you see them, pets, income, careers, and even the effect this person has on your heart and soul when you look into each other's eyes.

Include everything you feel or see in your mind's eye when you envision your life with this person.

Once you have the draft done, rewrite it until you have a perfectly clean copy with no spelling errors or cross outs—just this perfect letter that describes your life as if you were living it. Then read it out loud. Don't circumvent this step; it is important to read it out loud so you can hear the words.

If you stumble while reading it out loud, rewrite that section until you no longer stumble. You will find that stumbling means you stepped out of the clarity of the vision and into shoulda, woulda, coulda mode. When you are done, place your finished letter in an envelope and put it away.

I wrote my own letter with the help of my friend, Rose, more than a decade ago, and I found that letter the night before my wedding to my current husband, Jerome. My letter described our relationship perfectly. Our pastor used it during our wedding day—comparing my having faith in what I had written so many years before with Rebecca in Genesis 24 of the Bible.

Rebecca had faith that God would lead her to the man she was to marry, and she waited until she saws signs from God that that person was near. When Abraham's servant met her at the well in her small village, she knew he was sent by God. She had prayed (just like I wrote a letter as a form of prayer) and she was open when the answer arrived.

If you are willing to have faith that you can have all that you are meant to have, writing your letter can shift you out of your autopilot thinking and open you up to another possibility.

You can use this letter writing method for more than just relationships. Try it for your career, family, health, or anything you feel you want to shift into something it is meant to be versus something that does not fulfill you.

COMMUNITY

Community to me is made up of more than the physical community I live in. It is everyone I come in contact with on a regular basis: my wonderful hairdresser, Giovanna; my favorite restaurant, The Tides; my doctors; family; friends; neighbors; butcher; grocer; garbage men; Cheri, who gives the best massages in my town; etc. It includes everyone who is in my circle of influence and who places me in their circle of influence.

Inside my community, I want people to remember me as a generous, kind person who gave of herself so others could have a better life. My parents raised me to "give back for all that we have been given," and that is a foundational principle of who I am. Because of that, I believe that we all have something we can offer to others—whether it be our time, our expertise, our contacts of people we know, or even money. I tithe every year, and I also give to charitable organizations or people who can use whatever help I can provide.

Sometimes all I need to give is a smile to a random stranger. Try doing it. It is amazing to watch how one simple thing like a smile can change someone's day. I held a door open for a woman at my doctor's office, smiled at her, and told her to have a great day. She stopped, looked at me, and said that I totally changed her day and she was grateful. It was such a simple thing to do, and yet she was amazed that someone was doing it for her.

It is a shame that the simple courtesies I grew up with are now considered rare. When you say yes to someone, make sure you do so wisely and with discretion. I have been asked to be on many boards and fundraising committees, and have often been solicited by companies wanting free consulting or equipment when I owned my company.

When I first started receiving those calls and offers, I felt like I had to say *yes* to them all because they all had need—and I was awed that they would ask me. I just kept saying *yes*. I never asked myself any questions about the charities, or anything. I just said *yes*. After the fifth request, I realized that I would not be able to do my job or keep my company running with all the charity work I was agreeing to do.

I quickly starting asking myself a few questions, the first being,

- *Do I believe in the charity/community?*

Then,

- *Why do they want me?*
- *What can I truly offer them?*
- *What impact can I make for them?*
- *What will doing/joining this mean for the other things I have on my plate?*
- *What do I get out of being involved?*

These were very important questions because I realized sometimes these organizations really just wanted me to give money or products. They did not want me; they wanted their perception of how deep my pockets were. Others truly wanted assistance from me to help them have greater impact for their charities.

I learned that I wanted to be on boards that wanted me for me and not my pocketbook. If having my name associated with their charity helped further their cause, I would ask,

- *Does this relationship match my branding, or does it take me off track?*

It sounds a little self-centered, but look at what happened with Master Chef Paula Deen. She decided to link her name with a diabetes drug. Based on the negative press she got, it is clear that the public and the press saw this as a direct contradiction to her cooking brand. Time will tell if her cooking empire will recover to the same levels as before the announcement.

Personal branding is really all about your reputation and character as seen by the outside world. It is a visible reflection of what you stand for. Everyone has a brand, even if not in business. There is the stay-at-home mom brand, the employee brand, or the I-am-trying-to-find-myself brand. How you choose to let others see and perceive you will determine how they react to you on a daily basis. Just being a registered Republican or Democrat in the United States can affect how people believe you will react to a particular situation.

We need to be careful about how, where, and with whom our names are linked. Jane Fonda has still not gotten completely past the negative name of "Hanoi Jane" even with all the philanthropic things she has done since then. One unplanned photograph, taken innocently, was used to change how she was perceived by an entire generation.

You need to be careful with your personal brand as well. This is not to say that you should not link your name with something you believe in, but rather ask yourself the right questions instead of blindly saying *yes* to a request. You need to think through what it will mean in the short and long run.

I learned that if people needed money and I believed in them, I could write a check or help them with a fundraiser; but I did not have to agree to the time commitment of being on their board. Or perhaps there was a different charity I could link my name with whose focus hit more of the buttons that lit me up.

Today, I no longer make political contributions for all these reasons, because it puts me on lists that label me as that party's supporter even though I vote for candidates and not party affiliation. I don't want to be pigeonholed into a label.

Instead of donating only to a national charity, consider a local charity that may or may not receive funds from a national charity—which allows you a closer touch in your community. What about a local animal shelter versus a national organization—or the local Habitat for Humanity?

I love literacy programs that get books into the hands of children, and senior programs that get home bound seniors out into the world again. There are millions of charities out there. Try working with one in your community that aligns with your passions. This way, you are making a difference in your community and helping the organization gain additional funding or volunteer effort.

My mom has volunteered at a local thrift shop for more than fifteen years. The people she works with every week are some of her closest friends. As an added bonus I get some great one-of-a-kind items.

The big thing I learned around community relationships is that just because someone asks me does not mean I have to say *yes*. I learned to set my boundaries inside my community so that I can have the greatest impact while staying healthy. I have too many friends who spend all their time doing charity work to the point that they no longer enjoy it. They also never see their own families because they are always off doing some volunteer effort or another.

How involved do you want to be in the running of the charity? I also learned that I get really frustrated when serving if I cannot give input. So, in those cases where they don't want input but I want to help, it is best for me just to write a check. I am not good at watching people do things the same way over and over again when I think they could be getting better results with a slightly different approach. That's my opinion of course!

I take my board responsibilities very seriously. As a result, I am currently on the board of the Post Chapel in Vero Beach—a non-denominational chapel attached to the Indian River Medical Center. Right now, it is my only board position, but it is special to me as I have spent many hours praying there when I have had family and friends in the hospital.

I still donate to a number of charities and occasionally help with fundraising. In fact, the *What Would a Wise Woman Do?* book and speaking sales generate contributions to a fund I created which provides money to several different charities including the Michael J. Fox Parkinson's Foundation. By asking myself,

- *Why do they want me?*
- *What can I truly offer them?*
- *What impact can I make for them?*
- *What will doing/joining this mean for the other things I have on my plate?*

—and setting some personal boundaries with my time—I have been able to create a supportable process that will help a greater number of people while keeping my sanity.

As women, we always want to fix things, or make lives better for those around us to the point that we can forget about taking care of ourselves.

THE MOST FREEING WORD I HAVE LEARNED IN THE LAST TEN YEARS IS *NO*.

It is okay to say *no* to a request that will stress us out or reduce the amount of time we have for ourselves or our families, or one that we really just don't want to do. The most freeing word I have learned in the last ten years is *no*.

A friend of mine shared a dream she had one night. We had been talking quite a bit about setting boundaries with her mom, husband, boss, and friends. She had decided she was going to do it, and had begun speaking to her mom and others. As a result, she felt like she was more in charge of her own life.

The relief she felt was freeing for her and then she had this dream where she was running around peeing in a wide area all around herself. She gathered from the dream that she was like a dog or cat marking its territory. This dream disturbed her until it hit her: she was marking her territory by telling others what she needed!

Her dream let her know that she was telling the world, "This is my area; stay away unless I invite you in." The look of joy on her face when she realized the significance of the dream will stay with me for a long time.

Setting my personal boundaries has made me more available for the things that truly matter to me, and given me greater joy while doing them. How are you doing with your personal boundaries in your community?

BUSINESS RELATIONSHIPS

I used to think that business relationships were the easiest of the bunch, because in them you were only dealing with business matters. When I started working at age fifteen, I quickly learned that was so not true.

Business relationships are less about business than they are about relationships and emotions. (I wish they were more about business though.

I think they would be easier to navigate.) How many times have you heard someone use the phrase, "It's business, not personal," but being on the receiving end you said, "It is personal to me!" I know I have used this excuse on people myself and instantly regretted it. Yes, it is business, but we need to understand there are people involved too.

The next chapter focuses on business, so I am not going to go into much detail here, but I do want to say that I used to ask myself,

- What do I want to be when I grow up?

Now I instead ask myself,

- *What can I do with my life that lights me up?*

And then,

- *What do I need to do to fully achieve that?*

This is not about creating an image for yourself like a lot of the reality TV stars do. If you think that the cast of *Jersey Shore* is purely based on reality, then heaven help this world!

People often craft their public personas and have very different private ones. We only see what they want us to see. Dolly Parton is a good example. She has created a very distinct public persona with her wigs, clothing, fingernails, and stories, but she is also a very private person. She will tell everyone during an interview that her fans would be disappointed if they saw her in anything less than full "Dolly," so she never leaves home unless she is perfect.

This also allows her to have a very private personal life, because very few people know what she looks like without the wigs and makeup. I'd like to believe she looks even better, because I just love Dolly and the sunshine she spreads to me whenever I hear her speak or sing.

Recently, I was at an event where Frank Kern—one of the top internet marketers in the country—spoke, and he said that it is important to craft your public image, and then have everything you do or say be in alignment with it.

What I love is that he said you must be authentic with the image you present, because if you are not, it will fall completely flat—as no one can maintain an inauthentic public persona forever. Just look in any newspaper for the latest politician who has been in a scandal. Think Anthony Weiner anyone?

Let's take a look at some of my business relationships and decisions, and you will see where I was not authentic, and where I was. At times, I thought I was being authentic, but it was only because I was on autopilot. I was authentic to a point, but I was not conscious of how I was holding myself back until I realized where my choices were coming from.

?????
QUESTIONS TO ASK ALONG THE WAY

In regards to your circle, ask yourself:
- Who and what do I need around me to be a success?
- What in my life today is not helping me achieve my dream of being a successful business owner?

In regards to reality versus programming, ask yourself:
- Does the other person's reaction have anything to do with me and this situation, or is it about his or her history and fears?

In regards to finishing something, ask yourself:
- Why don't I want to finish this?
- What is stopping me from completing "xyz"?
- Will completing "xyz" move me towards my goals?
- Why did I start it?

- What are my expectations for what will happen when I finish…?

In regards to managing expectations, ask yourself:
- Was I clear and realistic with this person and with myself about what I wanted to receive?

In regards to having children, ask yourself:
- Do I want kids? Why or why not?
- Do I want them because I like being around them?
- Do I just want to have someone to take care of me when I get older?
- What does the warm feeling inside mean that I get when I hold babies?

In regards to asking why, ask yourself:
- Why am I doing this?
- Why do I want to do this?
- What can I do to change the outcome?
- Where can I get an answer?

In regards to pet ownership, ask yourself:
- Why do I want a pet?
- Am I prepared to make the time commitment involved with training, or am I better off getting an older pet that has already been trained?
- What kind of pet do I want—one I have to walk, or one that goes in a litter box or a cage?
- Am I willing to take on the responsibility for another being that relies on me completely for its entire lifespan?

In regards to friends, ask yourself:
- Do they challenge me to move forward or to stay where I am?
- Do they tell me the truth or the truth I want to hear?

- Are they successful at what they have chosen to do, or do they make excuses for why they fail?
- Am I the smartest person in my circle of friends?
- Do I dread getting emails or phone calls or running into these friends unexpectedly?
- How do I feel after I spend time with friend x?
- Are the friendships two-way relationships? This means, are they/ am I always taking or giving? If I am always taking, then it is time for me to ask myself why and stop doing that.

In regards to spouse or significant other, ask yourself:
- Why do I want to get married?
- Why am I doing what I am doing, and does it move me forward towards my goals I have for my future?
- Why do I have these goals? Are they mine or someone else's for me?

In regards to community or other commitments, ask yourself:
- Do I believe in my community?
- Why do they want me?
- What can I truly offer them?
- What impact can I make for them?
- What will doing/joining this mean for the other things I have on my plate?
- What do I get out of being involved?
- Does this relationship match my branding, or does it take me off track?

In regards to life or business, ask yourself:
- What can I do with my life that lights me up?
- What do I need to do to fully achieve that?

WISE WOMAN NOTES

Chapter 5

WHAT WOULD A WISE WOMAN DO? IN BUSINESS

"The purpose of life, after all, is to love it, to taste experience to the utmost, to reach out eagerly and without fear for newer and richer experience."
—Eleanor Roosevelt

WHAT SHOULD I DO WITH MY LIFE?

Do you love what you are doing? I mean do you have the jump out of bed, rush to work, smile all day, and struggle to believe the end of the work day is already here because it went so fast kind of love for what you do? Or, do you dread Mondays? Cringe when the alarm goes off? Procrastinate, complain, take long lunches, and only get happy when you realize it is Friday and you can leave? Do you dread Sunday because it means Monday is next and you have to go back to work?

If your answers to the majority of those questions leave you feeling anxious and exhausted versus joyful and full of energy, you are probably not in the right career or position. You may be really good at what you do and you might have even felt that you had a calling to do it, but if it does not make you want to get out of bed and tell everyone about it, that is a good sign that it is time to find what lights you up.

When I was a kid, the only question I asked myself about my career was, "What do I want to be when I grow up?" I never asked, *"Why do I want to do that?"* or, *"How do I get to do that?"* I wanted to be a cowboy, a doctor, an architect, and of course an astronaut. When I think back to *why* on any of them, my answer was the result of meeting someone who had passion and excitement for his or her job and made it seem like anyone who did not have the same job was crazy.

The doctor option was because my brother was sick and I wanted him to get better. A cowboy role seemed perfect because I loved jeans, cowboy boots, and horses. Architecture as a profession was because my dad was a builder, and I loved watching a new home go from design concept to finished house; plus I thought it would make him proud of me. And believing I wanted to be an astronaut was and still is because the idea of space travel and new worlds to explore and learn from fuels my spirit.

I first decided I wanted to be an astronaut when I was six. Growing up in the 1960s, men walked on the moon and circled the Earth for the first time. The space race was a race between countries, and the entire nation had a common goal of making it to the moon. When Neil Armstrong stepped onto the moon for the first time, I just knew I wanted to do that too. Because of that dream, I ended up studying computers and technology. I believed that was my only way to get into the space program short of the military, which was not for me.

The closest I have come to being an astronaut is living in Florida where I was able to see the shuttle launches from my backyard, and having clients who worked on the space program and served as the medical team for the astronauts. I have been fortunate to have cocktails with the head of NASA and several shuttle and Apollo astronauts as well. Now if I could only have met Sally Ride!

The dream of becoming an astronaut has enabled me to start and sell my own business, gotten me a newspaper column, fostered a love of science fiction, and led me to write this book. I may not have done what I set out to do—become an astronaut—but I have done what I was meant to do.

Along the way, I was passionate, bored, frustrated, passionate, disillusioned, and passionate.

I have often questioned my work choices and I continue to ride the roller coaster of emotions around work. I find myself more in the passion feelings as I refine my work focus to things that ignite my soul, rather than those that just feed the wallet.

Being an astronaut still ignites my soul, but that part of me wants the *Star Trek* version of space travel (all nations and people, regardless of race, creed or color or even planetary species work together for a united cause of exploration and increased peaceful knowledge and one in which our entire planet is united and prosperous), and our world is just not there yet. Perhaps I can ignite, through this book, one of you readers to create what is needed to make that happen as you open yourself to your true passion?

Bob Burg, multiple bestselling author of *The Go-Giver and Endless Referrals* and a highly sought after speaker on business, says, "Money is not the target. Money is what you get for hitting the target," and I have found this to be true in my life. When I focus on the money, it does not seem to flow into my wallet. Most times, it flows out. When I focus on what lights me up and results in others receiving something, I always seem to have enough money for everything I need or want.

As a child, my parents exposed me to many different ideas, cultures, and experiences. We rode horses. Well my mom and I did; Dad always pretended he was going to go, and then he always seemed to stay in the corral while Mom and I rode with the group. You would have thought my mom would have caught on by the fourth or fifth time.

We also played tennis, traveled, read lots of books on all kinds of topics, and talked to everyone we met. Things my parents loved to do or thought my brother and I might love to do were regular activities in our lives. As a result, my brother and I became passionate about pursuing our interests. Dad took us to explore open houses and visit historic homes, while Mom had us outside in the gardens or took us to the zoo.

As an adult, I still love visiting open houses, seeing historic sites, going to a library or bookstore, and wandering through a botanical garden; just don't ask me to keep a plant alive in my own home. A part of this book was even written at McKee Botanical Gardens in Vero Beach, Florida.

So what does all this have to do with being a Wise Woman in business? Lots. Understanding why you are making career choices and what lights you up is the key to staying passionate, versus dreading going to work each day. You need to stay open to what unfolds each day even if your experiences seem like they are running counter to what you feel you are supposed to be doing.

Opportunities and openings happen when and where we least expect them, and walking through one door will provide options you could not see from where you were on the other side of the doorway.

I've had a number of jobs and a few that were actually careers over the years, and I also had my own successful business. Each one gave me new experiences: some were frustrating, some were full of joy, and some were quite painful. The biggest lesson I learned from all of them is *know when it is time to move on, and when to move someone on.*

> ...KNOW WHEN IT IS TIME TO MOVE ON, AND WHEN TO MOVE SOMEONE ON.

I took my first "adult" job after college because the office was close to home, the salary was good, and the job was in my field of study from college: computer science and technical writing. It started three weeks after I graduated, and I stayed there for a couple of years. I enjoyed what I did. I worked with great people, had the freedom to contribute to how the group grew, and respected everyone I worked with and for. I never even considered leaving until I got a new boss.

Working for him was my first experience with discrimination for being a woman. You would think I would have encountered this before since I went to an engineering college, but I had not. I could no longer get any of my ideas implemented and I was relegated to proofing the memos my boss put out—which was made even more frustrating since it was a technical writing department and he could not spell and had even worse grammar.

What I discovered was the only way to get my ideas implemented was to have one of the guys in the engineering department bring my ideas up as if they were his own. To show you I am not kidding, I set up a test for the next meeting my boss threw. We knew the agenda in advance, so I told the men attending to watch for whatever idea I presented, and watch the reaction the boss gave me. If they thought what I said was good or even bad, I asked them to try to repeat it back exactly in a few minutes and watch what happened.

Every time I presented an idea to solve a problem being posed, I was passed over as if the idea had no merit. Five minutes afterwards, someone else would say nearly the same thing, and would be told by my boss, "Great idea. Let's do it."

I walked out of that meeting knowing there was no possibility of my career going anywhere within that organization with its current leadership. What would you do? I asked myself, *"Was the job worth fighting for?"* When I answered, it was with a *no*.

I realized I had done all I was going to be able to do there. Time to move on. I had no idea what I'd move to, but I sent my resume to a friend who had just left my company to work for another one. In five days, I had a better job for more money and better benefits.

The lesson I learned was that fighting for certain rights for yourself is not always the best use of your time. I'd encourage you to take the lessons you learn from those tough jobs you may have had and use them to improve your work and life. Sometimes you cannot win without changing positions. In that case, you just need to let go, move on, and move forward.

That was a hard lesson for me in business. It made no sense to me that others saw the problem but would do nothing. Office politics won out, and I was low on the political totem pole. That began many lessons for me on business politics and I think fanned the flame even higher that led to starting my own company a few years later.

With more companies downsizing and job security being up in the air right now for most people, I continually get asked how I made the decision to start my own business, what lessons I learned while I ran it, and would

I do it again. Because of those questions, I decided to focus this chapter on the entrepreneurial business person versus the person who works for someone else.

If you are working for someone other than yourself and are reading this chapter, a lot of the questions I pose throughout this chapter can be applied to any job you have, and may help you understand what your boss is thinking. That could get you that raise or promotion you want, or just make your job a little bit easier and more fun.

Should I Work for Myself?

Have you ever thought about running your own business—starting a business doing something you love and hopefully making money at it? Did you ever start a business and then realize that the business wasn't right for you? Did you not start a new venture because you were afraid to make the leap or take the financial hit to start? Do you want to start now?

My dad was an entrepreneur, and I grew up watching him through the ups and downs of owning and running a business with a partner. Granted, I did not understand a lot of what he was doing at the time because I was so little, but the idea of being in business for myself stuck in the back of my head.

After college, I worked for two companies before I started out on my own. One of those was a Fortune 150 company, and the other created products that were in hospitals all over the world to analyze blood. Did that mean that I was qualified to run my own company? Probably not, but I did have a master's degree in management, so I figured, *how bad could it be?* Plus, I had been working most of my life doing one thing or another on my own—including shoveling snow, raking leaves, and running the summertime lemonade stand when I was a kid to get money for things I wanted to do beyond what my allowance afforded.

You may not think of those childhood activities as working for myself, but they were a great foundation for understanding what is needed to make money.

In the last chapter, I mentioned that I took a separation package from the company I was working for that enabled me to have a nice buffer as I was starting my own business. I was also able to take advantage of a state program to add to my education by getting a grant for some technical training certifications. I was in an enviable position to start a business.

That is not always the case for everyone. The financial buffer wasn't the deciding factor for me though. I knew I needed to make a change in career because I had hit the ceiling at my previous company, both financially and intellectually. I began to feel there was no place for me to go if I stayed, plus I did not feel appreciated. I would get perfect reviews and no raise—not even a fifty dollar gift certificate to a restaurant or even a go-home-early-today pass. The politics were getting out of control, which meant I was stuck in the middle whenever I wanted to get even the necessary things done.

The tipping point was when my expense report got questioned over a ride home from the airport after six weeks in England working to complete a project. The only other things on the expense report were my hotel, meals, and car rental. Questioning me over something like that just did not make sense to me.

I realize now that my boss was responding to pressure to lower costs and do more with less, but at the time, I did not know that. All I knew was I was angry and frustrated that all they focused on was a one hundred dollar limo ride rather than the cost savings we had achieved with the successful completion of the project.

That was the straw that tipped the scales for me, and I am forever grateful. God (or the universe, the force, or whatever word makes you more comfortable) recognized that I was not going to move without a nudge, so He gave me the extra nudge I needed.

I asked myself at that moment,

- *Am I happy right now, this moment, with what I am doing?*

The answer was *no*. I then asked,

- *What would make me happy?*

The answer was setting my own rules. Those two questions I asked myself in 1994 were the birthing moment of Guardian Angel Computer Services, an I.T. services company with eventual offices and staff in Connecticut and Florida. I sold that company in 2009.

Starting that particular business was not a random choice. For years, I had been doing after-hours work fixing computers and helping friends set up their businesses with new technology. No money changed hands, but I realized I had a skill that was needed out there for small businesses. I also learned I had a talent for seeing what was needed before my "clients" did, because I was on the outside looking in to their businesses.

What does it mean to start and run your own business? It means learning how to think differently than you have been, which requires different questions than those you asked when you were an employee. Being in business for yourself is very fulfilling, but can be extremely stressful if you are not clear on who you are and what you want.

At the end of the day, there is no one to point a finger at other than yourself if you don't succeed. You can try, but if you are honest with yourself and are making choices you are not happy with, then it all rests in your hands, no matter how many employees you have.

If you are thinking about starting your business, it is essential to write down what you want to achieve, why you want to achieve it, how you expect to achieve it, and what you will do once you achieve it. So often we skip that last step because we really don't expect an end to our dream. I have found that skipping that last step keeps me on endless autopilot because I don't have an end destination in mind.

We've talked about how autopilot is not a good thing for your life in general, but at times, it can feel like a godsend to your business. About eight years into my business, we shifted from a wait-for-the-phone-to-ring model, to what quickly became known in the industry as managed services.

In a nutshell, we packaged our most popular services into three levels of pre-paid services, and offered them to specific clients at a discount. We were able to do this because newer technology was available that enabled us to lower our costs for doing preventative maintenance and monitoring of clients' equipment. We had to spend money up front to purchase the technology, but the technology would quickly pay for itself.

We began to see recurring revenue come in each month from clients, which enabled us to expand our product offerings and save our clients' money every month. That meant our operating costs were now covered each month, so we could leave that part on autopilot as we grew in other areas. We still needed to compare that portion of the business to our long-term goals and make sure we were still on course, but that part of our business began to run itself. We had reminders along the way to readjust as we saw things begin to shift off course.

It is much easier in many ways to work for someone else who handles the worry about payroll, business and employee taxes, operating expenses, vacation pay, etc., but even so, I have enjoyed working for myself much more. If you are deciding to go off on your own, make sure you hire a good attorney and tax accountant to set up your business, and begin a relationship with a local bank that will stand with you as your business grows. Strong ties to my community helped my business succeed even when we had our challenges.

Another part of starting your own company involves the decision to grow by adding employees, or to stay the size you are on your own. If you have written down the answers to your questions at the beginning of this section, you probably have an idea if this is a path you want to take or not. Perhaps you already have a company and are thinking about expanding. Or, maybe you work for someone else and have to hire a new employee. Let's take a look at what, for me, was a defining moment that changed the direction of my company.

TO STAFF OR NOT TO STAFF

When I started Guardian Angel Computer Services, the business was just me. No employees, no partners, no contactors. Just me. I loved it. I woke up each day, took care of my clients, controlled my schedule by allowing for time off—including hours I would see clients in a day—and set my rates based on what I felt my time was worth. I worked a lot of hours, but I enjoyed most every moment.

I was less stressed than I had ever been, and was making more money than I had been when I had worked for others. I also got to enjoy my dog, Max, and take five weeks off to hang out with my parents at their home in Florida over the Christmas holiday. I knew doing those things would limit my income, but that was fine because I actually was making more money while taking those breaks than I had while working under more stress for other people.

Eventually, I began to develop a reputation for quality work, and the phone rang a lot. I never advertised, but clients were talking about me and my business. Word of mouth had begun to build. This is the best form of advertising by far, and is priceless if you can get it. Never take it for granted though. Make sure you thank the referral source each time, even if you don't land that client—and ask that person what it was that made him or her refer you. Nurture that aspect of your business, and word of mouth will grow.

I realized I could reach more people if there were more of me than just me, so I started adding contractors. Contractors were great because I did not have to deal with payroll taxes, unemployment taxes, and all the other paperwork nightmares that having employees brings. Plus, I only had to pay them when they were bringing in revenue for the company.

That worked for about a year, until I got so busy I realized I needed staff whose schedules I controlled. Staff provided consistency for my clients, and a little less stress, I thought, for me. They also cut significantly into my profits because now I had overhead, payroll and vacation pay, and all the things employees expect and deserve. Plus, they expected to get paid and get raises no matter how the business was doing. Amazing, right?

My stress level was increasing, but I was still having fun; so I just kept riding the positive wave and not thinking about my stress or the business all that much. That wave is almost addictive. You think you cannot make a wrong step.

I've since learned that the moment I begin to click into autopilot and ride that wave is a critical time for me. That's when I need to become even more aware of what is happening around me. Otherwise, I become laser focused and can miss the small signals that indicate a course correction is needed.

I never asked myself anything significant when I decided to add staff. It just kind of happened. I didn't ask myself,

- *Where do I want my business to be in one year, three years, five years?*
- *How do I want my life to look?*
- *What do I want people to be saying about the company? What does my ideal staff look like?*

I never even asked,

- *Why do I feel I have to grow the company?*

That last question really opened my eyes after I sold the company and started to reflect on the fifteen years that were my life in founding and running the business. I had made a lot of choices because they felt like the right things to do or because they seemed like the easier choices.

In 1994, I was not designing my life and legacy with intent. Instead, I was on autopilot. My life and the way I wanted my life to be had changed, but I hadn't altered my course. My operating mode was all based on my beliefs around what it meant to be successful.

I felt the only scale of success that mattered was how big your company was, how strong the bottom line was, how many clients you had who were with you a long time, and the reputation you had in the community and press. Those are not bad barometers for a successful business. As a matter of fact, those are still the markers that business analysts look to while determining your business's worth. But over the years, I began to realize that my business felt kind of empty.

I loved almost all of my clients. They had become a sort of family to me, as had most of my staff. Since I spent sixty to eighty hours a week thinking about business, and working on and in the business, these people were pretty much my family. Because of this, it was harder to make shifts in my vision. I did not want to disappoint or hurt anyone.

Making business decisions only from that place cannot assist you in achieving your goals. Even though you don't want to, eventually you do end up hurting others and yourself because your frustration and unhappiness begin to take their toll and leak out in subtle ways until you reach a breaking point.

A big thing I learned about staff is when to let them go. Too many times I hired people because I liked them, even if they didn't really have the right skill set for the jobs I needed to fill. Other times, I kept people on because they had become friends—rather than because they were performing well. Because my staff had become family to me, my judgment was clouded at times. I began to realize I wanted to be liked by my employees even if it meant the business suffered.

Soon, I began to notice physical symptoms whenever I kept a staff member or even a client on too long. I began to dread going to work, I was always tired, and I had a short temper. I also realized we seemed to have more issues with a particular client that a "problem" employee served on a regular basis. When I would let a problem employee go or even just make the decision to let him or her go, I would feel relaxed, confident, happy, and free.

Even though I began to recognize this, I was never great at letting people go. It bothered me on so many levels. I learned that it needed to be done, however, because it was not serving anyone to have someone working for me who was not performing well. If you have employees and have ever asked yourself the question, *"Should I let him/her go?"* I encourage you to really look at that employee again. If you are even asking yourself that question, it probably means you should have let the person go months before.

I've been involved in numerous peer groups and been a consultant for several companies, and I have yet to hear any CEO say he or she regretted letting someone go for performance or attitude issues. More often I hear, "I should have let that person go sooner." The phrase, "Go with your gut," really means something to me.

When I would get quiet and evaluate my staff from my gut versus autopilot (which told me every hire I made was a good one and it was easier to just deal with whomever was already on staff than start the tedious and frustrating process of hiring and training a new person), this invariably resulted in improved morale, greater client satisfaction, and improved profits.

Sometimes, by letting someone go, you also are freeing that person to do something greater. One person I let go actually said he had felt unhappy with the whole industry for a long time, and was thinking of reinventing himself. I heard he was doing well in a non-tech industry.

You may be thinking that I recommend never hiring employees. That is not true. I do want you to understand the responsibilities involved with hiring staff though, and make a conscious decision versus just adding staff because you think doing so will help your business grow.

I have learned I am not a natural manager. I do treat people who work for me well, but I just assume that everyone knows what they need to do and will get their work done quickly and correctly. You can imagine that does not work very well since staff CANNOT read minds.

> ...STAFF CANNOT READ MINDS.

I've worked hard to change as a manager, but I came to realize that it would probably be better if I hired someone who is really good at implementing my ideas to direct the staff, since I don't enjoy that part of running a business. I cannot vacate myself from the process of the business, but I can bring in a good team to do the daily tasks in my next business.

If you are thinking about hiring employees, I recommend writing down what you feel your company needs in order to get it to the next level. That may include making changes to staff or products or sales and marketing or other things. Then determine why those things and staff are needed. Back in Chapter 4, I had you go through an exercise writing a letter as if you had the perfect relationship and were already living in it. This is a great time to do one for your business.

If you are thinking about adding staff, ask yourself,

- *What type of person would be best suited for that position?*
- *Would it be better to shift someone from a position he or she is in to another one, or hire a new employee?*
- *Can I outsource that position or use a search firm where I can try the person out as a contractor first?*

I created some powerful vendor relationships by outsourcing my accounting, twenty-four hour help desk, and product distribution to companies that were experts in those fields. My costs were lower, which saved my clients and me money. I also had less stress because I knew those companies would do everything possible to keep their skills up in order to continue offering me great value. Sometimes one less thing on your plate goes a looong way to fostering personal satisfaction.

If you still determine you need to hire someone, consider using an employment service that lets you try before you buy—and one that also vets the employees for things like background, drugs and alcohol, and past employment history. Using personality profile tools can also help find a good "fit" in your existing staff. I like *StrengthsFinder 2.0* by *Tom Rath*.

Make sure you have everyone in the company or team take the test so you can see what personality type would work well and effectively, and avoid rifts as you add personalities. A lot of successful business owners I know will not hire staff without first requiring them to fill out the DiSC profile.

DiSC was created by Inscape Publishing and determines personality profiles using a fifteen to twenty minutes series of questions that are answered online. There is a fee for the service, but it can be invaluable because it can foster quicker rapport and connection on a team. Like *StrengthsFinder 2.0*, it is just another tool in your arsenal that will help you understand what makes someone tick a bit sooner.

TO PARTNER OR NOT TO PARTNER

One of the biggest staff additions you can add to your business is a partner. A partner typically owns a piece of the business versus just getting a salary. A few times during my ownership of Guardian Angel Computers, I decided I needed to bring on a partner.

Go ahead. Ask me what I asked myself at the time. Absolutely nothing! Ask me if they all worked out. No. Did some of them? Yes. Why did some work and not the others? Dumb luck and asking myself better questions.

Remember earlier I said I did not do a lot of planning or thinking about where I wanted the business to go after I founded it? Well, all but one of my decisions to partner was another reflection of that lack of clarity. When I brought on my first partner, and then subsequently dissolved the partnership, I thought it would be better to bring on someone as a partner versus an employee, because that would make this person feel more vested in the success of the company.

There is an old saying, "There you go, thinking again." I never understood why that was a putdown versus kudos to someone. Thinking is good, right? Right. But only when you do so from a conscious place versus from an unconscious place. I really did not need a partner.

What I needed to understand was what I wanted for the business and for me—the type of people I needed on the team, what my expectations for each person were, and what things I was willing to give up controlling in order to move the company forward. That last one probably has you going, "Huh?"

Bringing on a partner or even an employee meant I was going to have to give up some control over aspects of the company. This happens when you add people, because you are no longer doing all the work yourself. If it is an employee you are adding, he or she is not your clone, so this person will do things differently. If it is a partner, he or she will have ownership and feel entitled to add a personal imprint.

If you are not willing to let that happen, it's better to just stay on your own until you know what it is you truly want for the business and your life. You can hire a general manager, chief operating officer, or other operational staff without giving them an ownership stake. You can create a framework for your business and require others to follow that framework, but be open to ideas they may have that can improve things beyond where you saw them going.

Whether you add an employee or a partner, make sure you have a great attorney who can draft employment and partnership agreements including clauses related to how the relationship will end, and what is required of each party in the event of a separation. Having those agreements didn't smooth out all the interpersonal issues that arose when some of my partnerships ended or staff members were let go, but it did create clarity on money, clients, confidentiality, and future competition.

I am forever grateful for my business advisors for making sure I was protected in spite of myself. They asked me during the contract process, *"If this goes bad, what do you want the end result to be?"* Sounds simple, but I did not want to answer, because I am the eternal optimist who did not see those relationships going bad. My dad, however, said, "Plan for the worst and then you can enjoy the best." He was a very wise man.

If you do bring on a partner, ask yourself,

- *Why do I believe I should add a partner?*
- *Will adding a partner move the business forward?*
- *Do I need a partner or a strategic consultant instead?*
- *What do I want this partner to be doing?*
- *What will adding a partner do versus adding an employee?*
- *Do I really just need a cash infusion for growth?*

If cash is the true reason you are looking for a partner, you can look into silent investors versus partners, business loans or grants, or perhaps a vendor partnership that provides you with the expertise and monetary inflow you need. You can even make the silent investor arrangement a short-term one, setting goals for buying him or her out over a specified period of time or giving "stock" on a future sale of the company. Make sure you have a good attorney to draft those agreements if you chose to go that route.

If you still feel bringing on a partner is the best decision, talk to others who have businesses with partners, and ask them what questions they asked themselves before the partnership was formed, and what they would ask themselves now. Find out how they found their partners, and see if they will share their partnership agreements. Talk to both partners if there is more than one, so you can see the situation from both sides.

ABC's *Shark Tank* is a great resource to help you figure out what you may truly want or need in a partner. On the popular and insightful TV show, budding entrepreneurs pitch a panel of successful business people on their ideas in order to get cash to move to the next level in exchange for percentages of their businesses. The bigger gain they receive, however, is in the expertise from someone who has the contacts, resources, and knowledge of how to grow a successful business.

Getting a "shark" to partner can launch a company into the stratosphere, or lead to giving up all rights to the company, because many discover that they are the reason the business is failing. I watched one episode where the founder needed to go if the business was to survive. Watch a few episodes, and then decide how your business is really doing, if you want to partner, and what kind of partner you may want to acquire.

I've learned a lot from watching other businesses and their leaders, and through personal experience, about how personal choices can stop a business from growing. It can often seem so much easier to keep hitting the wall with your head rather than stopping, looking around, and seeing if there is a better way to move forward. Sometimes making a change means taking a few steps backward so you can see how to go around or even go in a completely different direction.

I learned a valuable lesson during driver's education class in high school that made my business leap forward whenever I remembered to use it: always make sure you can see the rear tires of the car you are stopping behind. Doing so gives you space to make a course change if the other car cannot move, or if you realize you want to go a different way.

Stepping back and seeing the rear tires of what was in front of me—my desire for a partner—rather than moving forward quickly, would have reduced the pain of separating from the unsuccessful partnerships I forged. In other words, make sure you have perspective and aren't so eager to move forward that you put yourself in harm's way.

Each time I added or removed an unsuccessful partner, the business suffered monetarily, client relations needed soothing, and my time was consumed with legal matters. All of these consequences reduced the time spent growing the business.

In between partnerships, I joined peer groups that gave me the benefit of knowledge from people with more successful businesses than mine, and a sanity board that I bounced major decisions off of before making them. Sometimes I took their advice and sometimes I didn't.

In the end, decisions were always mine alone—as they will be for you if you are an entrepreneur. Once you bring a partner on, however, decisions are no longer yours alone. Choose wisely… and have a great partnership agreement, just in case.

To Sell or Not to Sell

One of the things I have found most entrepreneurs rarely think about is what happens when it is time to move on. We get so caught up our pride of ownership, hereafter known as the P.O.O. Factor, that we lose sight of when it is time to perhaps sell the company or remove ourselves from the daily activities. This especially seems to happen if it is our first company.

Why does this happen more on the first company you start? Your ego can get caught up in success or failure, and can cloud your perception of the realities of the business. I never had children, so Guardian Angel Computer Services became my baby. What parent doesn't have a blind eye for the shortcomings of his or her child?

When I sold the company, one of my staff members came up to me and said, "You okay? This had to be hard for you. I know you wanted to sell and the deal was a great opportunity, but this was your baby. Selling has got to be a little sad." Until he said those words to me, I didn't realize that there was a part of me mourning the loss in addition to celebrating the sale.

Once I had the awareness of the loss, I was able to fully process what selling my first company meant to me and to see more clearly how the actions I had taken along the way had determined its ending. Thank you, Greg, for providing me with that awareness.

REAL WORTH OR EGO WORTH

I had several offers to sell my company over the course of fifteen years, and one of those earlier deals actually went pretty far before we both backed out over the monetary terms. When I look back on those offers, I realize most of those deals fell through because of my expectations of what I thought the value of the company should be.

Either my ego got firmly planted in the way, or the other party's did. At one point my company had revenues of $250,000 for one year, and I told the potential buyer I wanted $1,000,000. Our profits were significantly less than that, but that amount seemed rational to me at the time.

That is what the P.O.O. Factor can do. That confidence can inflate your perception of the value of your company and keep you charting a course that may do more harm than good. When used well, however, it can help you achieve all your wildest dreams. The P.O.O. Factor allows you to have such unswerving faith in your business and decisions that you can push through any limiting factors.

The other thing, besides ego, that jeopardized some of the deals that came to my table was my staff at the time. I was of the belief that you let your staff know everything that is going on. I quickly learned that discretion is a key component of the M&A (mergers and acquisitions) process.

Letting too many people know what is going on around a sale too soon can hurt your business and ruin a deal. The first sale that we almost completed fell apart when we lost a large client because some of my staff had told a client our company was being sold. The client was concerned there would be instability during the sale process and afterwards, so the company did not renew its contract. The employees were under a confidentiality agreement, but they had violated it.

Once word gets out about the pending sale of a business, damage control needs to happen, versus focusing on the deal. That deal did not go through, and the employees I had at the time did not stay. Some of the staff felt I had owed them the first option to buy the company.

They had never spoken to me about that possibility, so the thought of selling them the company never even entered into my mind. Once they approached me about buying the company, I offered it to them for the same price as the outside offer. Neither deal went through, and eventually the unhappy staff left. The original deal fell through because word had gotten out and some key clients had left.

The initial deal had jobs for the entire staff, better benefits, and room for growth. To me, it seemed like a win for everyone. My perception was different than theirs. Perception is everything as evidenced by clients leaving even though the company that was buying mine was bigger and had more staff. People often just see a change and react from fear. Releasing sale information or even staffing changes in a controlled manner can deflect that fear and create opportunities for growth.

CHANGING PRIORITIES SHOWED REALITY

So what changed to finally make a successful sale of the company a reality? I began to turn off autopilot and truly look at the company as it really was (see *The Reality Point* from Chapter 1), including my staff and their performance, my performance as a business owner, and my clients. I stepped off autopilot and realized I needed to understand fully the value of my company from an independent, outside source.

As a first step to see clearly, I hired a firm specializing in business valuations. That outside valuation gave me the reality of how the company compared to others of similar and larger sizes. This assessment also detailed what could be done to increase my company's value. That process made me begin to see other questions I had not been asking.

I began to ask why some of the offers that came across my desk were lower than I would have thought they should have been, and why they weren't going through. A number of people came into my life who were familiar with mergers and acquisitions, and they began to show me that the only way to increase my company's value was to create recurring revenue (revenue that comes in each month on a contractual basis). That meant I had to change the primary sales model from "wait for the phone to ring." I had to restructure to sell blocks of time that would be paid for in advance and set up contracts with monthly revenues for specific recurring services.

FOR ONCE, IT REALLY WAS ALL ABOUT ME

I also learned, and believe me it was hard to hear, that the company had no significant value without me because its reputation was too tightly tied to me. If I ever wanted to sell the company successfully for a higher dollar figure, I was going to have to let go of the pride I had about my name being identified as being the company, and begin to separate myself from it. More about that last one in a moment.

DIFFERENT DOES NOT NECESSARILY MEAN BAD

A recurring revenue model was different from what I had been using, but it made a lot of sense. Changing my business model to monthly and quarterly contracts, and having staff do regular maintenance on computers, actually improved the quality of service we provided and decreased our customers' downtime (the time their computer systems and thus businesses were not operational).

This new model also enabled them to upgrade systems or put money into other areas of the business because their maintenance costs were lower. Who knew that increasing our sales would help our existing customers as well? This change meant we needed to ramp up sales to continue to bring on new clients, but that was all good as well.

One immediate change I made to ramp up sales was to ask myself different questions when presented with prospective clients. Rather than accept every client that came knocking or that was referred to us,

I evaluated them just like we evaluated any vendors we would consider adding on. I asked:

- *Does this potential client fit our ideal client model?*
- *Are we or they better served by passing this client along to another company better suited for their needs?*
- *Can I make money having this client?*
- *Am I ignoring any warning signs that indicate this could be a problem client?*

Turning down or letting go of some prospective or lucrative clients who were a drain on resources—because they were unwilling or unable to make changes to their systems or processes to improve cost effectiveness—was a huge step. This process cleaned and refined our client list. It also uncovered a vertical focus around healthcare we never realized we had. This enabled us to target market to that industry, landing us additional clients and setting us up as "experts" for that business segment.

I also learned to keep things closer to my vest on certain deals so as not to jeopardize them during the investigative stage. I began to do this with bigger proposals also so as not to let competitors know who we were targeting as potential clients. We started landing bigger clients and we developed newer contracts with our clients that allowed for a seamless transition when the final company sale happened.

Whether you are a business owner or work for someone, the questions above can help you focus the business and grow it. Sometimes the best client is the client you do not accept as your client. And the best deal can be the deal you walk away from.

At the same time, that lesson was only "part one" of learning how to change the way I had been running the business. Part two involved considering what was important to me personally. This part was harder because I had to decide how things had changed for me since I started the company. Asking this question required a lot of soul searching and conscious thought about the business and my needs, and whether I even wanted to do what might be needed to get to the next level and possibly sell.

I decided that rather than the company being my home, it would become my business. I would do what was best for me—then the company, my clients, and my staff. As a woman, I had typically put myself last, and I realized I had done that for years in my company as it grew. I had worried more about meeting my clients' and employees' needs than mine. Have you ever done that—worried about everyone else's needs before yours? There is a reason the airlines tell you to put your oxygen mask on first!

EMOTIONS IN BUSINESS: YES OR NO?

The feedback I had from the business valuation stated that the company would be more valuable if the association in the client base and peer community was not all about me. Changing the perception that the business was all about me was difficult.

Separating myself did not always go over well with clients or even some vendors who were used to contacting me directly for all the answers. I started to have staff respond to them instead of me, in an attempt to wean them away from feeling only I could help them. I was still in the background, but I added a layer.

My father had Parkinson's, and during the middle of all my business restructuring, I learned that his disease had escalated. My parents lived in Florida, and I had been building up a small client base near them so I could take extended trips to visit them and still have revenue flowing. My plans were to create an office there in time; but this was happening sooner than expected.

The progression of the Parkinson's escalated my plans and I quickly decided I was going to sell my home in Connecticut and move to Florida full time even if the business was not one-hundred percent ready for me to move. That would mean leaving the main office in the hands of others.

I thought I could run things from Florida, but I soon found out that would not work. What happened instead was I stopped paying attention to the main business, and got frustrated and angry when things did not move along like they had when I was in the headquarters office. Rather than deal with the issues—which would require me to step off autopilot and shake things up—I opted to ignore things.

At the time, it seemed easier to let things slide. Blinders can be a wonderful thing when you really don't want to see something. What I have learned is that the problem does not go away by ignoring it. It just gets bigger and bigger.

Blinders are just that—blinders to the reality. In the short term, they can allow you to move forward without the distraction of the things around you, but in the long term, they limit how far you can go. Blinders prevent you from seeing those other things around you that can help or harm you depending on your next moves. By the time you take the blinders off, it may be too late to make a correction in your business.

Look at race horses. Some of the horses require blinders to prevent them from seeing the horses on either side of them, because if they see the other horse or the starting gate they become too fearful to move forward. Remove the blinders and the horses are unable to run. Add blinders *and a jockey*, and these same horses run down the track with relative ease.

Each race is short though, and the horse has a jockey to guide it down the track. If you put on blinders, and don't have a jockey to guide you (read as keep an eye on the external factors you are blinding yourself to), you will probably bump into a few more things, possibly hurt yourself, and perhaps even lose the race. You may win, but it will be a more stressful ride.

In other words, blinders may suit the horse—who is not required to call the shots in terms of the next move to make—but they won't suit you as a business leader because you are in a long term race, not a short sprint.

As an entrepreneur, I ran my business alone and with partners. I thought bringing partners on board was like bringing in another jockey to run my race with—and sometimes for—me. I believed this other person would have the same end goal in mind and would think like me, but differently enough so that we would complement each other.

In the end, only one partner worked out perfectly for me. The other partnerships didn't work well at all, and in some ways hurt the forward motion of the business when I stopped guiding it. We may have had the same end goal in mind—a high value successful business—but the implementation was different for each of us, and these different approaches caused customer service and financial issues.

IS IT AN END OR A BEGINNING?

A number of factors led up to the ultimate decision to sell my company and take a short-term contract with the company that bought the business. The main decision, however, revolved around the realization that I was tired and was not being fulfilled anymore by what I was doing with my life.

If I had been filled with passion for the business, I would have happily done all that was necessary to bring the company to where I felt it should be with the right staff and client base. I would have happily commuted back and forth from Florida to Connecticut.

Instead, the thought of doing all of that made me want to lock all the doors in my house, turn off the phones and Internet, and crawl under the covers. That is not a good place to be in when you own a company.

The moment I decided to sell, I felt an overwhelming sense of peace. The entire sale process, from arranging a deal to all the legal issues to staff issues to client and industry full disclosure, took about eight weeks. My belief is that it was "meant to be," because I was ready to move on.

My move to sell proved to be fortuitous. I was able to spend a lot more time with my dad who passed away a year later—but lived to see me get married to an incredible man I met the weekend I decided to sell my company.

?????

QUESTIONS TO ASK ALONG THE WAY

In regards to business overall, ask yourself:

- Am I happy right now, this moment, with what I am doing?
- What would make me happy?

- Why am I doing what I am doing?
- How will I feel after I make "x" decision?

In regards to staffing, ask yourself:
- Where do I want my business to be in one year, three years, five years?
- How do I want my life to look?
- What do I want people to be saying about the company?
- What does my ideal staff look like?
- Why do I feel I have to grow the company?
- Should I let him/her go?
- What type of person would be best suited for that position?
- Would it be better to shift someone from a position he or she is in to another position or hire a new employee?
- Can I outsource that position or use a search firm where I can try the person out as a contractor first?

In regards to partners, ask yourself:
- If it goes bad, what do you want the end result to be?
- Why do I believe I should add a partner?
- Does adding a partner move us forward more than I can without one?
- Do I need a partner or a strategic consultant instead?
- What do I want this partner to be doing?
- What will adding a partner do versus adding an employee?
- Do I really just need a cash infusion for growth?

In regards to clients and growth, ask yourself:
- Does the potential client fit our ideal client?
- Are we or they better served by passing the client along to another company better suited for their needs?

- Can I make money having this client?
- Am I ignoring any warning signs that this could be a problem client?

WISE WOMAN NOTES

Chapter 6

What Would a Wise Woman Do? In Times of Personal Crisis

"Never get stuck on stupid."
—General Russell Honore

Why Is This Happening to Me?

Have you ever asked yourself that question when faced with a personal or family crisis? I know I have, but I have learned to ask it from a learning perspective versus a victim perspective. From a victim perspective, the question is more like, "Woe is me. Why do bad things keep happening to me? I didn't do anything to deserve this."

With a learning perspective, I learned to ask,

- *Can I take control of the situation?*
- *Is there one thing I can do right now that shifts the response I am getting, or makes the result a better one right now, this moment?*

I much prefer living in the learning perspective instead of the victim perspective. Let's go back about twelve years ago to a lengthy run I had of some pretty bad health situations.

ARE YOU WAITING FOR OTHERS TO GIVE YOU ANSWERS?

The room was quite cold as I sat waiting for the doctor to come in. It felt like I had been in doctors' offices more than anywhere else over the last year. Now, I was waiting for yet another doctor—this time the chief of infectious disease for the hospital—to come talk to me. He was a specialist in Lyme, and everyone was leaning toward that for the reason why my physical and mental health was falling apart. I couldn't understand how or why this could happen to me.

When he finally came in, however, I was in for a surprise. He told me he thought I was sick because I was depressed due to not being with a man. My friends could not believe I let him live. I chose not to accept that diagnosis. You see, I wasn't going to get stuck on stupid and that was what his diagnosis felt like to me.

A month or so later, I saw another specialist who actually listened to me and reviewed my entire chart before he even examined me. We reviewed my case files, and saw my blood work had been misread. I was suffering from Babesia—a tick-borne illness—and Lyme, and he felt the disease had started to affect my brain chemistry. Depression because I am single, my ass!

Learn to read your own blood work. That was the biggest lesson I got from that day. It is a relatively easy skill to learn at a basic level. The Internet has great information that will teach you that skill.

Learning what the tests all mean will enable you to ask better questions of your doctors. Plus, I have found a number of doctors only look at the blood work to see if you are in range. They don't look at trending. This may lead to problems being caught later in their development rather than earlier when it is often easier to correct them.

Doctors are not infallible. Sometimes they have not run across your particular situation. Or, because they are so busy, they might not have read about the latest new option or natural method for reversing a disease. The more information you have about your own health, the better conversation you will have with your doctor.

That one lesson I learned from being misdiagnosed ended up preventing a number of later misdiagnoses of family members. Doctors always ask me if I am in the medical field because of the quality and depth of the questions I ask. The knowledge I have gained and the ability to phrase things in their language creates a two-way conversation about health versus a one-way interaction.

Early on in my dad's Parkinson's diagnosis, he asked me if his doctor would get mad if he brought in the questions I had prepared for him. I told him, "If you doctor gets mad because you are questioning him, it is time to change doctors." If we had listened to a few of my dad's early doctors, he would never have stood up again after he broke his hip, and he would have died a few years earlier than he did.

I had never been really sick prior to that run-in with a tick. Yes, I had all the usual childhood illnesses plus a bout with pneumonia and Epstein Barr, but none of that had affected my brain. The Epstein Barr had made me exhausted all the time, but I was still able to function on a daily basis by reducing the activities I did and by resting a lot.

I had known something more serious was wrong with me, but it was difficult to get someone to believe me. All too frequently, doctors look at women and say, "Just get some more rest," or, "Here is a pill to make you happier." In the past, I had managed to push past and through illnesses. They slowed me down a bit, but never stopped me. This one, however, was stopping me and I was angry.

I was angry and full of emotions that would well up out of nowhere and affect my daily interactions with others. I was:

- Angry that something I could not see was stopping all my plans for my life.

- Angry that I could not get someone to believe there really was something wrong and that it wasn't fibromyalgia.
- Frustrated that all I wanted to do was sleep and never leave the house, even though sleep didn't give me any relief.
- Concerned because my memory was failing me on the simplest things, which was affecting my business and ability to function for even the most basic things like boiling water for tea.

Hint: Get a whistling tea kettle...I destroyed a number of pots before I discovered whistling tea kettles. My mom didn't believe in tea kettles, so I never had one in my house growing up. Until I learned a new way of thinking about tea—using tea kettles that whistled—I burned a lot of sauce pans!

In total, it took close to a year from when I realized I was really sick until I found the right doctor who was able to diagnose me and get me on the correct treatment. During that time of failing health and going from doctor to doctor to doctor to doctor, I went from:

- Why me?
- Are they right about me?
- Am I going to die?

To:

- *What is wrong with me and what do I need to learn to heal myself?*
- *God, send me whatever and whomever I need to be healthy and thank you for the lessons I am learning.*

The *why me* question never seems to get me anywhere other than self-pity—and the accompanying chocolate cake and ice cream pity parties. This only starts a vicious cycle of weight gain and sugar crashes, so other than a quick emotional spike from the chocolate, I always end up crashing even lower than where I started.

I have found what works best for me is to ask myself:

- *What can I do to change what is happening right now, this moment?*

Then, when I have changed the moment, I can see a possibility of a future that is better than what just was.

Personal illness, family illness, and financial illness can be so overwhelming that our whole lives just seem to stop moving in any direction. Even our autopilot feels like it stops working because we often have no reference point to work from anymore.

While I was going through my personal health crisis, every aspect of my external life that I believed just seemed to work without any thought on my part at all began to fall apart. I stopped almost all social engagements including business networking events, dinner with friends, movie nights, and even making phone calls when I got home.

Anything I did became a spontaneous event versus a planned one, since I did not know hour by hour how I would feel and whether I would be capable of functioning. I was just too tired and in too much pain to fight my way out of the fog.

Routines I thought were permanently etched in my brain, like driving back and forth to the office, didn't even work anymore. I put my car keys aside because I could not always remember what to do when I was driving.

I was in a depression, but I learned my depression was due to the illness and the medicines I was taking causing a chemical depression. Once they supplemented my serotonin, I began to engage more. Staff and friends actually commented that I was smiling again! I had not even realized I wasn't smiling anymore—my nickname in college had been Smiley.

Have you ever experienced a time when you could not remember how to drive home from your office? That experience gave me a new perspective on what it must be like for a dementia or Alzheimer's patient. I would even forget what I was saying mid-sentence—not fun when you are trying to land a major client to keep your business going.

Post-it Notes became my friend. I had to write everything down immediately, or set timers and reminders on my computer so I would not forget important things like appointments, food cooking on the stove, and phone calls I needed to make.

My parents moved in with me for a few months to drive me around and take care of basics as I was healing. That time was precious to me, especially because it was shortly after we discovered my dad had Parkinson's.

Once my illness was under control and I was off the medications, I was able to get off the antidepressants. I began to experience a new version of normal. I also took homeopathic serotonin for a while as I weaned off the drugs. I am grateful to my dear friends Sue Graves and Keith Alstedter who taught me about natural ways to heal my body and mind. They were always there to support me. It helps to have friends.

I don't wish what I went through on my worst enemy, but you will probably be surprised to hear that, looking back, I value that time. I was more in the moment than I ever had been, because I had no other choice. I pared my life down to what was important at the time, and dropped a lot of other things. I had even considered selling my company at that time and had a potential buyer, but it was not meant to be.

This time was incredible because the illness made me begin to look at what I really wanted in my business and my personal life. I began to realize during that sick time that how I was living wasn't working anymore. I was living for work. Most of my extracurricular activities were work related— either charity events or networking. I did hang out with friends, but mostly at business events.

I found out who my true friends were during this time, and who were the ones really hanging around for what I could do for them. My true friends helped me get through each day. They supported me when I began to rebuild my business. Some even offered to fly to Connecticut to help me cover client projects when I realized my staff were not working the way the business needed and that I needed to hire new staff.

I have to say that it is painful to start over this way, but it is like ripping a Band-Aid off quickly. The pain is over in an instant, and then there is only a vague memory of the pain with new skin growing underneath to protect the area from harm again.

Personal illness can seem like it is only happening to you. But that is just you closing down your outside view and putting on blinders because it seems easier at the moment to get through it. Besides affecting you, illness also affects your family and the community around you.

My parents drove up from Florida to take care of me for three months—all because my office manager answered the phone when they called and told them I was in bad shape. I hadn't wanted to tell them because I didn't want to worry them. (Thank you, Jennifer. I think you helped save my life with that one phone call.)

A part of me had been thinking I could beat the illness on my own, and that it would pass quickly. Once my parents arrived and I had help at hand, I learned I had been exhausting myself beyond the mere effects of the physical illness.

From that simple gesture on Jennifer's part, I realized I needed to ask for the help I required. Asking for help was not something I was comfortable doing. I could help others without a second thought, but to ask for something I needed seemed like admitting a weakness.

When my parents arrived, they were curious why I hadn't wanted to tell them how bad I really was. I told them I hadn't even realized things were that bad. I had been deceiving myself—which I later learned was also part of the depression I had from the Babesia and the drugs I was on to kill the parasites in my blood.

My parents raised me to be strong and do whatever was needed to get things done. I had learned to be self-sufficient, but I forgot their other lesson: it's okay to need other people.

During the worst part of the illness, I had been asking myself, "What is wrong with me? Why can't I get better?" Instead, what I needed to be asking myself was:

- *What do I need to do to get through the next day?*
- *Who do I know or need to know that can help me?*

- *What questions do I need to ask myself and my doctors to get well?*
- *What do I need to change in my life that may be contributing to my health issues?*

Those questions took me out of myself and gave me permission to not have all the answers. They also opened the door to the possibility that I could get well and take an active role in changing my health. I had been the victim of my illness with the old questions.

With the new questions, I took control of my attitude and mood. Eventually, I got the right doctors and medications and made lifestyle changes to move me forward with my health.

I find it difficult not to have all the answers. Not having all the answers means there is something out of my control, and that means something could go wrong. Most of the women I know have this same need to have all the answers.

I am learning that you ultimately have more security when you don't try to control every detail. By letting go of the need to know all the answers, you open the door of possibility for new ideas and answers—sometimes ones which are much better than those you might initially imagine.

When you don't have all the answers, you switch into learning mode and off autopilot. Learning mode provides new questions, which often lead to the answers you need versus the answers you want. Sometimes you are lucky and the answers you want are the answers you need, like *the cancer is curable,* or *it was just a shadow on the x-ray,* or *give it a week of rest and your foot won't bother you anymore.*

FAMILY ILLNESS

Did you know that more caregivers are women than men? According to a 2011 report by the AARP, two thirds of all caregivers are women (see http://www.aarp.org/relationships/caregiving/info-07-2011/valuing -the-invaluable.html). This doesn't include those who take care of their husbands, partners, children, jobs, and themselves on a daily basis. As women, that puts a lot of stress on us which we tend not to think about. I had never really thought about how cumulative stress can affect us.

In the past two and a half years, I sold my company, got married, had my dad pass away, tore two discs in my back, had a husband and mother go through open heart surgery, and changed careers. I just kept on going through it all, and then I started to hurt all over. I began to worry that the Babesia was back and that I was in for that whole health ride all over again.

Turns out it was not the Babesia, but stress taking its toll on my body. I just refused to believe it. Then some friends of mine said, "Laura, *where and when do you feel best?*" I realized I could not answer that question. Even going to the beach wasn't relaxing anymore, because I felt guilty about all the things I wasn't getting done. I believed I needed to be taking care of someone else before myself.

I started thinking about when that trend started. My brother died from a congenital heart defect when he was thirteen. I was just ten years old, but I knew my entire life that Robert was different from other brothers. For one thing, he had a pacemaker and could not be in my grandmother's car when the radio was on. If you turned it on, it would change his heart rhythms in a bad way. In today's world, this would not happen due to technology improvements, but back then, a random radio could send him to the hospital if we did not catch the interference to his pacemaker in time.

I took on the responsibility of protecting Robert from anything I thought could harm him, because I didn't want him to die. Looking back, I see how this hyper-vigilance set up patterns in my life that still stand today. I worry that if I don't pay attention to everything going on around me and try to control my world, something bad might happen. Do you recognize that story in yourself?

STOP, IN THE NAME OF LOVE…WELL NOT REALLY

As a child, I actually stopped doing things I loved because my brother could not do them, and I didn't want him to be upset by seeing me do them. I never asked him if my doing things he could not do bothered him; I just assumed they would.

Have you read, *Life's Golden Ticket,* by Brendon Burchard? I love how wonderfully he writes about this exact issue. Now, instead of self-inflicting emotional pain on myself because of what I assume someone else wants or needs from me, I ask others directly what they need or how they would feel if I did or didn't do something. Almost every time they say, "Please don't stop because of me. I want you to do all you can and be all you can. It makes me sad when you don't do things that you can do." Ask yourself:

- *What have I stopped doing because of what I think someone else will say or feel?*

> JUST BECAUSE SOMEONE ELSE CANNOT DO SOMETHING THAT YOU CAN DOESN'T MEAN YOU SHOULD SUPPRESS YOUR JOY AND PASSION.

Just because someone else cannot do something that you can doesn't mean you should suppress your joy and passion. Think about the four-minute mile barrier that existed in running. Before Roger Bannister ran the mile in less than four minutes in 1954, the world believed that feat was impossible. After he broke that barrier, many other runners quickly followed his example.

Family illness stopped me from doing things at an early age. I am not, however, the same young girl with a sick brother today. I can choose to live differently.

Family illnesses are not unique to me, and likely not to you. They happen in families all over the world on a regular basis. Cancer, accidents, heart disease, Alzheimer's, and Parkinson's are just a few that I know on a deeply personal level.

As I write this book, my mom is recovering from open heart surgery for three heart valves and a blood clot, and my husband had a triple bypass eight months prior to mom's surgery. In 2010, my dad passed away after a fall brought on by Parkinson's disease. I don't talk about this so you can have pity on me for everything that I have been through over a short period, but rather to show you there can be a light during crisis if you are willing to look for the blessing.

I learned a lot watching my dad progress through the stages of Parkinson's. Throughout it all, he kept a smile on his face and rarely lapsed into *why me?* questioning. I know he struggled because he was always such a physical man. We all struggled with his illness. But we learned to find the blessings, too.

If it wasn't for my dad getting Parkinson's, I might not have met my husband. I moved to Florida because of my dad's illness, and my new neighbor, Susanna, introduced me to Jerome. Five months later, we were married and Susanna was my maid of honor. That was a wonderful silver lining.

WHAT? ME, *WORRY?*

In some ways, the worrying and hyper-vigilance has taught me incredible things and helped me learn better questions to ask. In doing so, I have been able to prevent the preventable. In other ways, however, worrying has stopped and hurt me by preventing me from taking chances sooner.

Most worry is about tomorrow, but all worry is experienced today. Since worry takes up your energy today, it often stops you from actually living your fullest life. Worrying means you are living in fear of what might be or what others may think, and not living your fullest life. You miss a lot when you spend your life in worry.

Dictionary.com defines worry as: *to torment oneself with or suffer from disturbing thoughts; fret.* I've learned that worrying cannot always prevent illness, but worry does stop me from being present to the people I love during the crisis. I have spent so much time trying to resolve everything I could that I was not always there to hold the hands of my loved ones when they felt scared and alone.

The most enlightening and life transforming question I learned that helps me release some of the worrying was recently brought back to my attention by my friend Tina:

- *Can I change it?*

If you cannot change a situation by anything you can do or anyone else can do, you need to let it go. Give the problem to God or place it wherever you have to so you can find peace.

For me, I have learned to give my problems to God. Doing so is a constant struggle because I always feel there must be something I can do, someone I can connect with, or something I can learn that will make a difference in whatever I am worrying about. When I remember to ask myself, "Can I change it?" I find I spend more time living than worrying.

Due to all the personal and family crises I have lived through, I have spent a lot of time in various hospitals and doctors' offices. If you find yourself in those situations and are uncertain how to proceed or even where to go to find out if you need to worry, try a few of these questions:

In the hospital, ask:

- *May I speak with the charge nurse?*

This is really helpful if you feel the care being given is not up to par. My dad once felt like the nursing aide wasn't doing his job well. Dad was afraid to say anything because when he did say something the nursing aide made Dad feel threatened. Since he was bed bound as a result of a fractured hip, he essentially was in fear that if he asked for help, he would get hurt by this aide.

I found this out and called for the charge nurse who immediately switched the team assisting my dad. As a result, his care and mental attitude changed significantly. We later found out that the aide was let go. The hospital had felt there were issues, but no one had been willing to give concrete information. Once they had our report, they were better able to evaluate the aide and let him go so no one else would ever feel threatened while helpless.

That was an extreme case, but asking that one question immediately shifted my dad's situation for the better. Here's another good question to ask:

- *What medications do you have my (insert relationship here) on and why?*

We tend to trust the medical teams working on our loved ones, but it is important that we understand and they understand that we are an active part of the healing process. I knew my mom was allergic to one drug they were about to give her, but somehow the allergy never made it into her medical record at the hospital. I spoke up, and the crisis was averted.

Knowing the drugs a patient is on can also help you understand the reactions they may have so you don't worry needlessly. It is beneficial if you have medical power of attorney and/or if the hospital and doctors are given permission by the patient to talk to you as they are held to several federal regulations around patient privacy.

Here's another helpful question:

- *Is there anything I can do that will help you give better care to my....?*

Nurses especially love this question because they are often overworked. The most common answer I've heard is, "Spend time with your loved one and make him or her laugh." You of course need to let the patients heal by getting rest, but keeping some signs of normalcy helps them heal better.

I also help with meal times and bathroom visits if the staff allows. Plus, I always bring food for the hospital staff working the floor my loved one is on as a thank you for all they do every day to help those we love. Chocolate, fruit, cakes and pretty much all things homemade are always a hit.

In a doctor's office, ask:

- *How much experience do you have treating the illness you just diagnosed?*

Sounds simple, but depending on the illness, you may be better off working with a more experienced doctor as the primary medical lead rather than the doctor who came up with the diagnosis. A fresh set of eyes can lead to options, but sometimes they can limit the options as well.

When I was undergoing treatment for Babesia and Lyme, my medical team was up-to-date on all the latest research and treatments. We were able to use both Western and Eastern treatment options to speed my healing. If you don't live in an area where you have a lot of options, see if your doctor is willing and able to present your case to other doctors that he can work with.

Also ask:

- *What are the side effects to the medications, how long has the drug been used for treating the illness, and are there any alternatives?*

Dr. Mehmet Oz is a big proponent of food as medicine to reduce or eradicate certain diseases. My husband recently went vegan to get off medication for Type II diabetes, and has been successful at making that shift. He stayed on the medicines until the doctor said he could eliminate them.

Sometimes medicine is the best answer but it is important to have all the facts. A good doctor will work with you on the options you have. Some just want to prescribe drugs because it is easier. Use the Internet to help you ask better questions of your doctors. If they get mad, and some will, find another doctor who is open to a two-way conversation about your health.

Ask:

- *What will I be billed for?*

Have you ever asked your doctor what it would cost to see him? You probably have if you do not have insurance, but most people who have insurance just don't. I encourage you to check first. I have had friends ask this question before they had a procedure done or a drug prescribed, and they learned that their share of the procedure or drug was something they simply could not afford. The follow-up question is:

- *Is there another option?*

Often there is, especially with medications. It pays to know your options even if the option you are given is that there is no other option.

Hospital stays and medical bills are a major fear for a lot of people, and have forced a number of people into bankruptcy. They are not something that can always be planned for, and therefore asking what your options are and knowing in advance what the costs may be may help alleviate fear and reduce worry. Knowing your costs and treatment options beforehand will help reduce the unknown component of your health crisis.

Don't be afraid to ask for help. Your doctor can often put you in contact with organizations that provide grants for patients in need. You don't have to do it alone. That is why so many local and national organizations exist. They want to help.

If you are feeling overwhelmed by a diagnosis for yourself or a loved one, seek out someone to talk to. Perhaps your church, the chaplain at the hospital, a patient advocate, or a local branch of whatever illness you were diagnosed with can guide you or just listen. You are not alone. Even your pharmacist can help.

Money, or the fear of not having enough money, is one of the top ten concerns most people have. When you add another top ten fear of illness to that money mix, it is enough to stop most people in their tracks—which is why the next chapter is devoted to money matters.

?????
Questions to Ask Along the Way

In regards to personal crisis, ask yourself:

- Can I take control of the situation?
- Is there one thing I can do right now that shifts the response I am getting, or makes the result a better one right now, this moment?
- What is wrong with me and what do I need to learn to heal myself?
- What can I do to change what is happening right now, this moment?
- What do I need to do to get through the next day?
- Who do I know or need to know that can help me?
- What questions do I need to ask myself and my doctors to get well?
- What do I need to change in my life that may be contributing to my health issues?
- Who can help me?
- Where and when do I feel best?

In regards to family illness, ask yourself:

- What have I stopped doing because of what I think someone else will say or feel?
- Can I change it?
- May I speak with the charge nurse?
- What medications do you have my *(insert relationship here)* on and why?
- Is there anything I can do that will help you give better care to my….?
- How much experience do you have treating the illness you just diagnosed?
- What are the side effects to the medications, how long has the drug been used for treating the illness, and are there any alternatives?
- What will I be billed for and is there another option?

WISE WOMAN NOTES

WISE WOMAN NOTES

Chapter 7

WHAT WOULD A WISE WOMAN DO? IN MONEY MATTERS

"Worry often gives a little thing a big shadow."
—**Swedish Proverb**

WHAT DOES MONEY MEAN TO ME?

Do you worry about not having enough money? Do you have fear even though you have money in the bank? Would others in your position be angry at you for worrying, because they don't have anything close to what you have in the bank, and yet still you worry? Do you worry about spending money so much that you ration to the point of frugality, and then indulgently splurge on things you really don't need or even want?

If you said yes to any of those questions, welcome to my world. I did not grow up with lack. We traveled as a family every year to wonderful places. We took day trips on Sundays, went out to dinner, went shopping (a favorite pastime for my mom and I), and gave to charity. We had a nice house, in a nice neighborhood, and we had nice cars.

When I turned sixteen, I got the family station wagon—a 1969 Ford Torino Squire station wagon—baby blue with fake wood panels on the side and a yellow sculpted shag rug in the very back section! Life was happy and wonderful, and yet for some reason I developed this fear that I needed to save money for "some" day. I had a driving feeling or belief that "the other shoe will always drop and you need to be prepared."

A PENNY SAVED

I remember the first time I opened a bank account. I was five years old, and the bank came to our kindergarten class to talk about savings and money. They encouraged us to open an account. All you needed was a penny back in those days, and they handed you a bank book that showed all your deposits. Did you have a bank account when you were five years old? I'd like to think that was a good thing, since I have had the other shoe drop. Those savings have carried me through health and business lows.

When I think about money, I tend to get pretty stressed. Even when I have a healthy bank account balance, I fear that the balance will go lower and not higher—even when I know that to be untrue.

I'm writing this chapter sitting in a park along the Intracoastal Waterway in Florida. Across from me is a multimillion dollar home with a sixty-foot yacht at its private dock. I had this image in my head for most of my life that when I could live there, I would have made it. It didn't even matter to me whether that person was in debt up to his or her eyeballs. All I used to see was a perception of success and a life that would be stress-free and happy.

Is that really what they have—joy and peace? What makes that a more stress-free life than living in a mobile home, tent, or condo?

When I finally got quiet with myself and stopped the striving to get that house, I asked myself:

- *What is it about that life that I want?*
- *Why do I want it?*
- *Is my striving for that (fill-in-the-blank) my need or someone else's?*

I became aware that I associated living on or near the water with having made it all the way to the top of the achievement ladder. I thought anyone who could own a home on the water had achieved success in his or her respective career and could finally take a break.

Today, when I see that house and the boat, I realize I am looking for a place to rest from the stress of my life. I want a place that I can go to anytime and feel how I feel when I am sitting in this park.

But I can do that now. I can go to the park and not have to pay the large taxes or payments for upkeep on that house. Or better yet, I can close my eyes and bring up the vision of that house or this park and feel my body relaxing immediately.

Success, monetary stability, and freedom mean something different to everyone. For me, I realize I have fears around money so I continue to learn new ways of shifting my thought patterns to more positive ones that reflect what money and success mean to me. The way I first did this was to write down what I believed my idea of success was, and then I questioned where that belief came from. Was it truly right for me?

What is it for you? Take a moment and write down your idea of success. Write out a vivid picture of where you would live, what your life would be like, how you would feel, and what your friends would be like. This is similar to the letter you wrote in Chapter 4 on relationships. As I had mentioned, this type of writing really works well in all areas of your life and business.

Once you are done, ask yourself:

- *Why is this the way I define success?*
- *Where did that vision of success come from?*
- *Does this picture represent my belief about success, or is it someone else's that I adopted?*
- *Is there another way I can feel successful without all the material trappings?*
- *Does that belief serve me and my future?*

Rewrite your letter as necessary after you have applied the above questions. You may be surprised what the new letter says. For me, I learned that a walk on the beach or sitting near the water in the middle of a work day can instill that same feeling of peace and success.

I still want the house, but the striving feeling of stress and fear about never having enough money goes away when I acknowledge that it is better to have the feeling of success and security within me all the time, rather than waiting for that feeling to come from the external world's reinforcement of me as having "arrived."

I still want the house and the boat—but because they are beautiful and I like being surrounded by beauty—rather than because I think those things define success and happiness. The water soothes me and is one of my definitions of beauty—along with a child's smile, a rose, sunsets and sunrises, and clouds that look like dogs. You may have different definitions. Embrace them. Just make sure they are your beliefs and not what someone else has told you is beautiful.

My parents were raised during the Great Depression in the early thirties. They knew "want." I never did, but they taught me early on to save early, spend wisely, shop for a sale, and never pay retail. Even if you can afford retail, why pay it? Those things you think you need to have? They will go on sale tomorrow!

Those lessons have come in handy throughout my life, but somewhere along the way I developed guilt over having when others didn't. It has been very hard for me to see others in need and not give them money, even when I wasn't paying myself in my business. I still felt I was better off than them, and I needed to put them ahead of myself. I often forget that airline warning: put your oxygen mask on first when it comes to money and a few other areas of life.

Bestselling author Melissa Tosetti of www.TheSavvyLife.com says in her book, *Living the Savvy Life,* that anyone can have the money to live his or her dreams; it just requires making choices throughout your day and having a goal in mind. Are you making goal-focused choices in your financial life, or are your finances dictated by ever-increasing debts, wants, and desires for more and more things? Is the need for immediate gratification preventing you from having that house on the waterfront, the new car, or finishing your education? Ask yourself:

- *What are my financial goals?*

Several former clients have had employees embezzle funds from them. One client had that happen twice. When I asked how it happened, the client said, "I stopped paying attention to my money and allowed others to take care of my financial future." When I asked the client how it had happened the second time, she told me that everything had been going really well. But then she went on autopilot and just assumed everything was still going well, until checks and cash payments began to disappear.

Finally, she realized she had been working hard, but her bank balance didn't reflect her efforts. All the checks and balances they had put in after the first embezzlement went out the window when she was lulled into trusting the second person.

I am not saying that given the opportunity, employees will embezzle. Not at all. The majority of people are ethical and honest. What I am saying is that you are responsible for your financial success and failure. No one else. Only you can achieve your financial goals by conscious decision making and concrete goal setting for your future.

You may have setbacks due to unemployment, underemployment, and the recent mortgage fiasco, but at the end of the day, you make the choices as to how you spend and save your money. No one else. Yes, unexpected things come up like illness, job changes, home repairs, etc., but those can also be planned for by creating an emergency or rainy day fund.

My parents told me to put aside a minimum of ten percent of my salary each pay period into an account that I did not touch. When the emergency finally came, I had money in the bank to cover medical bills, home repairs, etc.

It takes time to build up that emergency account. If you don't have ten percent right away, start smaller. Look at your expenses for a month by writing down everything you spend, and then see if there is anything you can do without to save for the bigger picture.

PIGGY BANK SAVINGS

My husband takes all the dollar bills out of his wallet each day and puts them in a jar. He also empties his pockets of all the loose change and puts those in a giant size Hershey's syrup piggy bank we got at the Hershey's store in Hershey, Pennsylvania. It's a very chocolaty place to visit! We recently deposited the money from his dollar jar and there was more than three hundred dollars inside.

It is an easy way to start saving because dollar bills and change tend to get spent on a lot of incidental or unplanned purchases like coffee, candy, ice cream cones, and so on. If you remove them from your wallet and pockets each day, you will find that you are less willing to break larger bills for those kinds of expenses—thereby saving yourself money. Ask yourself:

- *When I think about money, how does it make me feel? Do I get stressed? Do I feel calm? Do I think about all I can do with my money, or do I immediately think I will never have enough money for what I want to do?*

All the experts tell you that to have financial success you must spend less than you make. That is true, but what if instead of just saying to yourself, "I must spend less than I make," you say, "I want 'x'—so 'y' is really not important compared to 'x'?" You will still be saving, but this time for a goal versus just saving for the sake of saving.

LAUNCH WHEN READY!

I can stick to something for the long term if I see and feel the benefits and end results in my mind and body. Are you this way as well? Rather than just beating yourself up for spending money, shift your thinking to set up spending priorities. Decide what is important and write it down. Here is my money priority list in no particular order:

- Tithe ten percent a year minimum.
- Have a home on a large body of water with no mortgage—and money saved in a separate account for at least five years' worth of tax, insurance, and upkeep payments.
- Take at least two vacations per year paid for without using credit.
- Own a car I love with no payments.
- Have enough money in the bank so I can pay all my taxes, insurance, etc., after I retire.
- Be able to donate to charities that move me, and be able to take time off to assist them.
- Be able to buy what brings me joy without guilt or without worrying the purchase will bankrupt me. (Make sure whatever you are purchasing is what will bring you long term joy. An instant gratification purchase will soon be unused and cause regret in the future when you look at it and ask, "What was I thinking?")

I do have my crazy dream list, if money was no object, and so does my husband (an Audi R8 convertible for him and a trip to the international space station for me); but for now, I have things that I want that are more important. Ask yourself:

- *Have I written my list yet of what I want and/or need?*

Have you tracked and written down one month's worth of expenses? I mean everything including money put in parking meters, gas, tolls, coffee, groceries, tithing, charities—everything you spend money on including your existing debt. I have a template you can use on <u>www. WhatWouldAWiseWomanDo.com</u>. It is a free download and can help you get started.

If you haven't started yet, run a quick inventory in your head of recent purchases so this next section will make more sense. But really, just grab a pen and paper or a keyboard and computer and start gathering the info.

Now look at your spending habits for a week, a month, and the past year. Do those spending habits help or hinder you in achieving your financial goals? If they help, see how you can increase them. If they hinder, stop each of those habits that don't serve you. If you can't go cold turkey on your spending habits, or they include items you cannot eliminate right away such as paying off debts, figure out how you can work towards reducing them.

One example might be transferring credit card balances to lower interest cards and seeing what money you can shift from one area of your budget towards paying off your debts. One thing that jumped out really quickly for me when I did this exercise was I realized I was stopping by Starbucks pretty frequently for my favorite grande hot chocolate no whipped cream.

A Starbucks hot chocolate cost me around three dollars per cup. I really didn't need one. I could make my own, or get one once a month. It had started to become an unconscious habit, and I really didn't need to be drinking all those calories either.

I still choose to go to Starbucks, although much less frequently because it really is the best hot chocolate I can get next to a little shop in San Gimignano, Italy—yum! How much could you put into your emergency fund or that vacation you want if you cut back things like outside coffee, or hot chocolate in my case, to once a month or less?

Some people I know stopped going out to lunch and were able to save $300 per month to put towards credit card debt. They still had lunch, but they brought it from home at a much lower cost. That simple change in habit gave them an extra $3,600 per year they didn't have before.

If you don't have debt (Whoo hoo, congrats to you! Go get a Starbucks hot chocolate!), but you have other goals, wouldn't $3,600 per year get you that much closer to having that vacation or car with no payments? It may mean you can buy fresh vegetables over frozen, or get new tires for your car.

With a few other changes—like carpooling to work, planning meals to take advantage of groceries on sale, shopping in your own closet to find clothes you forgot all about, and having potluck dinners at home with friends versus going out to a mediocre restaurant—you can more readily achieve your financial goals.

I have some wonderful financial advisors who have helped me save for the long term, and I highly recommend talking to and hiring someone to assist you if you have never had any financial training. But, at the end of the day, the choices you make around how you spend your money are what determine if you have enough for everything you want and need.

Over the course of my life, I have made some really bad investments because I took someone's advice without question. I've since learned I need to ask more questions about investments. One broker made more than me on stock trades because of his commission. He had me buying and selling stocks constantly, and I never realized how much he got each time a trade happened. I lost quite a bit of money while working with him until someone pointed out to me what was going on. It was a great lesson though.

Ted Turner of CNN fame is one of the wealthiest people in the United States, but he lost more than eighty percent of his wealth with one business deal that today is still considered one of the worst business mergers ever: the AOL/Time Warner marriage. He could have blamed everyone else for that loss, but what he did was pick up the pieces and start moving forward again towards his financial goals. He realized they went into the deal not fully prepared, and he paid the price in the end.

What I have learned about money is that worry does not increase my bank account. Instead, it often leads me to impulsive purchases and subsequent lack because I am afraid to take chances or search out new ways of increasing my funds.

What works is voicing why I am afraid, and setting goals (preparing to the best level possible) to reduce or eliminate the fear. "Spending less than I make," is a wonderful rule to live by, but I like to add to that by saying, "Spend on what will give me long term joy rather than short term gratification." Ask yourself:

- *Am I making long-term or short-term money choices?*

TODAY, THIS MOMENT, IS A FRESH START.

Look again at your expenses for the last six months and decide your answer to that question. Congrats if you made choices you still feel good about. If you didn't, don't get mad at yourself. Today, this moment, is a fresh start. Everything changes right now for you if you choose your future, over the moment, when making money decisions.

?????
QUESTIONS TO ASK ALONG THE WAY

In regards to a penny saved, ask yourself:

- What is it about that life that I want?
- Why do I want it?
- Is my striving for that (fill-in-the-blank) my need or someone else's?
- Why is this the way I define success?
- Where did that vision of success come from?
- Does this picture represent my belief about success, or is it someone else's that I adopted?
- Is there another way I can feel successful without all the material trappings?
- Does that belief serve me and my future?
- What are my financial goals?
- When I think about money, how does it make me feel?
- Have I written my list yet of what I want and/or need?
- Am I making long term or short term money choices?

WISE WOMAN NOTES

WISE WOMAN NOTES

Chapter 8

What Would a Wise Woman Do? In Self-perception

"Stay inside your best self."
—Diane Sawyer

Is Someone's Opinion of Me My Reality?

When you look at yourself in the mirror, what do you see? Do you see a beautiful, talented, successful woman (or a man, if you were a man brave enough to pick up a book titled, *What Would a Wise Woman Do?* and read it)? Or do you see someone who is fat, unattractive, a constant or perpetual failure, or perhaps even unlovable?

Never mind that you make great money and are the perfect weight for your size. Never mind that you have the respect of your peers or are even a supermodel, business tycoon, or mom. Often what we see in the mirror has no basis in fact. The image is instead our self-perception that has been warped by circumstances from our past, and the beliefs of people around us.

Scott Carbonara—a speaker and author who formerly served as an award-winning crisis counselor and later an executive chief-of-staff of a multi-billion dollar company—stated to me in an interview, "Be careful who you let hold your mirror. If the person holding your mirror doesn't see you as you want to see yourself, take your mirror back. Similarly, reflect the light for others—and like a houseplant growing towards the light, others will seek your leadership." (See his blog at LeadershipTherapist.com for more ideas.)

What we believe about ourselves could have been developed as the result of a one-time casual comment we misunderstood, or a decades-long environment of physical or emotional abuse. It does not matter the cause; what matters is how we reacted to it and are still reacting to it, and how it has limited or impelled us forward.

We can allow ourselves to be controlled by our thoughts, or we can control our thoughts and turn them into positive motivators to propel us forward to our best futures. One of my favorite quotes is from Siddhartha, the founder of Buddhism, *"We are not what we think we are, but we are what we think."* I love that quote because it reminds me not to believe all the voices in my head.

OUR EXTERNAL SELF-PERCEPTION

When I was a little girl, I was told I could not go for ice cream with my brother because I could get fat. Robert was always painfully thin because of all the heart surgeries he had to undergo. But I was not. It was not that I was fat, but I had definitely started to gain some weight. Whether it was from baby fat, emotional eating, or rebellion because Robert could eat anything he wanted while I couldn't, I will never know. All I know is ever since, I have been a frustrated eater.

I remember vowing to myself that day that no one would be able to stop me from eating anything I wanted once I learned to drive. See, once I could drive, no one could control my eating—because I could go get whatever I wanted whenever I wanted. Occasionally, I still find myself getting in my car, eating whatever I want, and sometimes hiding the fact I did.

Each time I stopped for that hot chocolate I mentioned in Chapter 7, I was treating myself to a fattening treat that would have been frowned upon or commented about when I was younger. When I started thinking about why I kept stopping to get a hot chocolate I realized that I went there every time I was feeling stressed or frustrated about something. Then I would make a point of throwing the cup (evidence) away before I got home.

It was bad enough that the stop to buy the hot chocolate was an emotional fix versus a conscious choice. Hiding the evidence I had ever been there from my family made it seem like it was even worse. There was no enjoyment over it versus having the cup of hot chocolate or a gelato with my husband in Italy—because in Italy the hot chocolate was a joyous, nurturing public experience with my husband. It was not a Band-Aid to suppress the emotions I didn't want to feel.

My self-perception around weight had been molded from a casual comment made when I was little. My parents always told me I was beautiful, but weight was and still is an obsession in most of the females in my family.

And my family is not alone. In Mauritanian culture, it has been considered desirable for a woman to be obese. That is changing slowly, but for generations girls would be force fed to make them fat. We have the reverse in the United States: thin is in, and the thinner the better. There is a movement to be healthy versus fat or thin, but all the marketing out there still shows unrealistically thin women as the ideal we should all try to achieve.

I admire women who don't obsess about their weight, and still feel great about themselves and are healthy. At least from what I can see from the outside looking in, this seems like a healthy way to live.

Being healthy has now become my goal; I would not mind having less weight because it would be better for my health. I've put some practices in place to get there. Today, for example, I ask myself,

- *Will this piece of candy make me feel better in the long run or just the short run?*

If I answer short, I try to understand what I am feeling that has me wanting the short-term fix of the jelly beans or chocolate cake—or a New

York bagel with homemade chopped chicken liver. (I will always be that New York girl from the Bronx no matter where I live!)

WIN FROM WITHIN

For me, food is connected with emotions. I am, however, learning to unlink food from unhealthy emotions. I feel physically and emotionally better when I stop eating sugar, gluten, and dairy. It is a struggle for me though. I have not yet found a replacement food or activity that gives me the same emotional feeling as a perfect margarita, warm piece of chocolate cake with Andes peppermint chips, or even a toasted bagel with butter; but I am learning to ask myself why I want those foods and how they will make me feel in the long run.

The technique for achieving health is similar to what we talked about in Chapter 7 regarding money. It is okay to pick the short term fix occasionally; but if we do that all the time we will run out of money. In the case of health, we will run out of it too if we always choose short term emotional food choices over the longer goal of wellness.

We win when we act from within and understand why we are making our choices. This means that we are on a path to winning because we are choosing what is best for our whole selves, versus reacting to outside influences and patterns of learned behaviors that do not serve our future and present selves.

I would love to hear your ideas for healthy, tasty replacement beverages and foods. You can reach me at www.WhatWouldAWiseWomanDo.com. I don't think I am alone out there in wanting to live a healthier life!

DO YOU HAVE ANTS?

I am not talking about the insect kind that always seem to come in packs and leave me feeling crawly and itchy all over even after they are gone, but the mental kind that Dr. Daniel Amen talks about in his bestselling book, *Change Your Brain, Change your Body.* Dr. Amen talks about the ANTS in our brains.

ANTS are those Automatic Negative Thoughts we all seem to have that create fear, negativity, and anxiety. They can even stop us from living a healthy life. Come to think of it, maybe the ants on the ground are a perfect analogy for the ANTS in our brains. They get in everywhere, are difficult to kill and prevent from coming back, and consume your thoughts while you are trying to get rid of them in your "house." I really don't like ants of any kind.

When we allow the ANTS to become the predominant thoughts in our head, Amen suggests journaling what is running through our heads at the time. By bringing conscious awareness to those negative thoughts, we take control back in our brains. If we don't acknowledge the thoughts and determine where they come from and why, we cannot change them.

He really is talking about taking yourself off autopilot. Once you gain awareness of any automatic behavior pattern, it immediately begins to shift its hold on you. My mom recently had open heart surgery. The weeks leading up to her surgery were like torture to me. I was afraid to leave her alone because it might be the last time I ever saw her or heard her voice. I spent every moment I could with her. When I wasn't with her, I was an emotional wreck.

Heck, when I *was* with her I was an emotional wreck. I was eating every bad thing out there, I was not sleeping, and even prayer was not working to soothe me. I tried a few cocktails, cake, Rescue Remedy, and even a few Xanax when I had a panic attack. It wasn't until I went to church, saw the prayer team, and started uncontrollably crying that I finally asked for help from them.

One of the women asked me to consider,

- *Why am I letting fear rule me?*

She said, "Stop filling your mind with all the images fear brings up and start filling your mind with visions of a successful surgery and a joyous outcome. You have no control over the situation anyway. You are killing yourself with the stress your mind is putting you through."

What a wakeup call to the ANT running through my brain! We prayed and a peace began flowing through me. I went home and journaled around all the worse case scenarios I could come up with. Then I went through them, figuring out what I could change and what I couldn't.

If I couldn't change anything, I just let it go and gave it to God to handle. This worked for me. I had to keep repeating the exercise every time one of those thoughts resurfaced in my head, but I spent much more quality time with my mom and husband after I cleared those evil ANTs out of my head. My friend Koya reminded me to do it again recently when I was stuck in a loop and unable to write. It worked again. I really need to keep that lesson at the top of my mind.

Consider adding this exercise to your bag of tricks you keep handy to look through every so often when you are feeling overwhelmed or find yourself looking in the mirror and judging yourself.

IT'S A SLIPPERY SLOPE

I recently went three months with no sugar, gluten, or dairy. It went really smoothly because I had a goal of a healthy body and mind. One day, I realized I had not lost any weight while restricting my diet, and I started thinking another one of my long-time ANTs of, "Well, why bother then?"

Can you guess what happened next? I ate some jelly beans and bread and a few other things. Shortly after, my weight was up; but worse than that, my body hurt. I had allowed my negative self to control me again. I went immediately back to old behavior patterns because it was much easier to eat gluten, sugar, and dairy than it was to prepare healthy meals or find a restaurant that could serve me.

All of these examples from my own life are all ways I have seen myself. I've struggled to hold my own mirror. For example, I have always seen myself as fat even when I was a size four. Even when I ran a successful company, part of me said I was a failure because I didn't have a bigger, *more* successful company.

When I got divorced, I did things that proved my ex-husband's comments about me to be true. He wasn't in love with me or attracted to me because he felt I was fat. I took that comment he made and built it into a belief that I was not attractive and I was unlovable. As a result, I did everything possible to make people love me—including making business decisions that were not in my best interests all to make the other person think I was great.

Because I was always insecure about my body image, that negative thought inside my head of being fat and therefore unattractive and unlovable took firmer root and grew out of proportion to the reality of my body and soul.

MIRROR, MIRROR IN MY MIND

Our visual perception of ourselves is a major issue for most women. Men don't seem to have this issue as much as we do. As women, we often judge ourselves more harshly than others judge us. I have not figured out why we do this yet (and would love to hear your ideas as to why), but what I do know is we can choose to stop letting the outside determine our self-worth.

When I coach my business clients who are trying to grow or start their businesses, or when I talk to clients who are having some personal crisis going on, I always start them off by asking themselves and answering the question,

- *Who am I being in my business or in my life—and is it really who I really am?*

If you are not being true to yourself in a situation, it will always cause you problems—whether those problems show up immediately or a little bit down the road. I was talking to someone who recently started her own business selling handbags. She said that she wished she could be like her mentor who holds incredible handbag parties and has so much energy and excitement.

You need to understand that I know both these women and their personalities could not be more different. One is an effortless extrovert with a huge personality—a Martha Stewart type. The other is a quiet, tiny Southern woman with an inner quietness to her that catches your attention. You just want to be around her and absorb some of that quiet.

How could the quiet one expect to become the extrovert and maintain that all while starting a new business? Answer: she can't. I advised her to be herself and find what works for her. Not everyone responds well to a particular personality. What works for others will not work for her because she will be working so hard to maintain a fictitious persona that her joy for the new business will not shine through.

When she started talking about the handbags in her own language and with her own style, you could see the smiles, joy, and love for the product beam through. It almost made me want to buy another handbag. She will attract a different buyer than her mentor, and that means an overall greater market share for handbag sales. How is that a bad thing?

So what if you have always thought you were being true to yourself, and then you noticed that what used to work for you no longer does? As time moves forward, you will change as well. Who you were at eleven, twenty-one, thirty-one, forty-one, fifty-one, sixty-one, seventy-one, or even eighty-one may not be who you are now. As you learn, grow, and shed what no longer empowers you—or as you let go of outside forces that blurred the total you—what works and what is true for you may change.

I was an avid sports fan when I was younger and while I was in college. I was even a baseball sports information director for my college. This was an unusual position for a woman to hold at the time, but I enjoyed it and it paid for the rest of my college education. After graduation, I still followed baseball and football to the point of paying crazy prices for fifty-yard-line seats for Giants playoff tickets for myself and my then-boyfriend.

If you are not a sports fan, just play along and go, "Wow, she must have really loved sports! Those are expensive yet really awesome seats."

As I began my business career, I realized that I had learned to love sports and single malt scotch because my dad had told me that to compete in a man's world and get my foot in the door to move ahead, I needed to learn to drink scotch, play golf, and talk sports. After you got your foot in the door, he said, it was the rest of what you knew that kept you there.

He was right, because more business was done after work or on golf courses than in business meetings. It was great advice, and to this day often enables me to get a conversation started in business deals.

In the process, however, I learned that I really did not care about sports. I do like single malt scotch, but I don't drink much anymore. My golf days are also over due to a back injury, except for the rousing miniature golf games where I battle the windmills!

I changed as I got older, and playing the "game" of business does not make me feel good anymore. I find I only want to do business and be in relationships with people who are open to what I really have to say and to the truth of their businesses. I am grateful for my dad, because he taught me what I needed to play in a man's world.

I owe a lot of who I am as a business person to my dad and his guidance; but as the world changed and my dad was no longer in business, his rules no longer applied the same way. He was right in that you needed to learn and use what got your foot in the door, but it was no longer just sports and golf and scotch.

The day I realized that I didn't need to pretend to love sports was wonderfully freeing for me because I didn't have to enjoy or do those things any more. I could still talk about them, but it had begun to sound false in my own ears. It was more of a struggle to fully participate in those conversations. I now prefer talking about business strategies, the latest book I read, or spreading the word about a tool or technique I have learned for reaching deeper into achieving my greater purpose.

Sharing those things light me up and isn't bad for a career as a speaker and consultant either. They also make me a better person, because I am being honest about who I am with those around me. Ask yourself:

- *What do I believe about who I need to be in my business? My marriage? My family? My friendships? My community? My life?*

Write down your answers, and then review them and ask yourself:

- *Do they reflect who I really am inside?*
- *Do I enjoy being that person?*
- *What would happen if I shed aspects of my personality that don't reflect who I am today?*

Sometimes we find that habits we've developed don't suit us in where we want to go. When I graduated from college, I used a lot of cutting remarks and banter that I had adopted while traveling with the athletic department. In order to survive in locker rooms or on athletic fields, you had to give as good as you got—and often before you got it given to you. That did not work so well in a business environment.

My officemate at my first job mentioned that I busted chops a lot, and was curious why. Since I wasn't really that person in the first place, I realized I did not have to be that way anymore to fit in and thrive. My environment had changed; but I had not changed to shift with it. Once I did, I felt better, and my relationships began to thrive. That was a wonderful lesson for me about how environment can shape your responses.

Changing self-perception can work in two different ways: you can shed a behavior that does not work anymore, or add a behavior that does. I like to use the Grinch from Dr. Seuss's *How the Grinch Stole Christmas* as the perfect example of someone who learned a new and positive behavior. He learned to love when he had never done so before. He became open to what was not working anymore, and his life changed dramatically as a result.

You could say that he shed a behavior that was not really him—being mean—and took on a behavior that did—love. I see it as this: he grew to the point that what served him before no longer served him.

When you wrote down your list earlier in this chapter of who you believe you need to be in your various relationships, what did you discover? Ask yourself:

- *Is there anything I need to let go? Why?*

How about something you want to add to make something better than it was? I realized I needed to become a better listener and not try to "fix" everyone's problems when I did this exercise the first time. Now I ask people,

- *Do you just need me to listen, or do you want advice?*

Sometimes, people just need to be heard.

I'd love to know directly what you are changing and why. You can email me or post on the forum at <u>www.WhatWouldAWiseWomanDo.com</u>. I have found that by hearing what others go through, I'm often sparked to make changes in my life. It creates an opening in my thinking that might not have been there before. When I am listening, my autopilot stops because I am learning something.

Diane Sawyer's quote at the beginning of this chapter has stuck with me because staying inside your best self means understanding who that best self is and growing even better as a result. Ask yourself:

- *Who is* my *best self?*

?????
QUESTIONS TO ASK ALONG THE WAY

In regards to self-perception, ask yourself:
- Will this piece of candy make me feel better in the long run or just the short run?

In regards to ANTS, ask yourself:
- Why am I letting fear rule me?

In regards to mind mirrors, ask yourself:

- Who am I being in my business or in my life—and is it really who I am?
- What do I believe about who I need to be in my business? My marriage? My family? My friendships? My community? My life?
- Do they reflect who I really am inside?
- Do I enjoy being that person?
- What would happen if I shed aspects of my personality that don't reflect who I am today?
- Is there anything I need to let go? Why?
- Do you just need me to listen, or do you want advice?
- Who is *my* best self?

WISE WOMAN NOTES

Chapter 9

WHAT WOULD A WISE WOMAN DO? IN SEARCHING FOR FAITH

"When all else fails, there's faith."
—Unknown

"I must seek to see from God's perspective rather than my own distorted human outlook."
—Henry Blackaby

DO YOU BELIEVE IN GOD?

That seems like such a simple question as I look at it, but that one question triggers so many more for me. It seems to do that for a lot of people as well. The "God question" triggers more arguments, wars, hurt feelings, family rifts, and misguided actions than any other that quickly comes to mind for me other than politics.

I have been all over the map when it comes to my spiritual and religious beliefs, and I know I am not alone just based on the numbers of books about God and religion that exist. Just go to Google and type in "God." When I did it, more than 1.85 billion listings came up!

I was raised Roman Catholic, but we were not regular weekly church-goers. We went at each holiday, but it was difficult for my brother to be in the crowded church so we often skipped services. I enjoyed it when I went—until they switched from Latin to an in-the-round mass in English. I think mostly I disliked it because it seemed less mysterious to me at that point.

My personal journey to find what or who God is began in earnest in 1973. I told you about my brother, Robert, who was sick. My whole world changed overnight when I went home from a friend's house, expecting to greet my brother as he came home from the hospital as usual. He was not there. I could feel that something was different when I walked into the house that morning.

I remember running down the street to get home, excited to see Robert. As I got to the bottom of the stairs, I realized the house was silent. It was like there was no air. Patches, our dog, was not even waiting at the top of the stairs to greet me. Then I saw my mom's face and I knew something was wrong.

The lack of air in the house moved into my lungs and I could not breathe. I did not believe them when they said Robert wasn't coming home. I figured he just needed to stay in the hospital a few more days. When it finally hit, I felt empty—like someone had walled off all my feelings inside. I couldn't even cry anymore. I just shut everything down and wanted to get back to my life as I had known it before Robert had died.

I had no answers, and neither did my parents. I just wanted to know why Robert died, and why the doctors hadn't made him better. No one had any answers other than, "It was his time to go. God wanted him, and he is no longer in pain." That was not very reassuring to a ten-year-old.

I kept asking God and my priest, "Why did you take Robert away from us?" All I heard was the answer of silence during my prayers. So, I did what any ten-year-old would do: I got angry with God and didn't speak to Him very much. In fact, I started exploring a lot of other religions and spiritual paths over the next thirty years of my life. I went in search of answers that I felt I was not getting from the God I grew up with.

MAY THE FORCE BE WITH YOU

I never lost faith that there was something out there bigger than me. Even wanting to be an astronaut, I felt science could never explain away how the Big Bang started. I mean, who created the material for the Big Bang anyway? Arthur C. Clarke even wrote a short story about a crisis of faith and the universe in his short story, *"The Star."*

Every spiritual path I studied gave me a new and deeper awareness of myself, the world around me, and how we are all connected at a very basic level in our daily needs and cares. I consider this our soul connection.

Recently, after years of consideration, I went back to calling that "bigger thing" I had been searching for God. It feels right to me because I feel Him as a personal presence in my life now versus an external idea. To this day though, I still catch myself calling Him "The Force" or "The Universe" in addition to God. Seriously, I do.

When *Star Wars* came out in the seventies, it was like George Lucas was talking directly to me and filling a void that formed when Robert died. I loved the idea that we were all connected, and that what we felt and did to others was able to be felt around the world.

I also thought it would be really cool to be able to move things with your mind and prevent fear from controlling you. Plus, it meant I could still talk to Robert even though he had moved on from an earthly being.

I felt there could not be a God after Robert died, because why would he do that? Why would he leave me alone? My ten-year-old self was hurt and afraid and felt alone, and didn't know how to ask for help. I didn't know what I needed other than my brother back. I wanted God to take me instead, so that my parents could have their son back. I wanted Dad to have the son to follow in his footsteps.

That part is actually kind of funny, because my dad was a builder and a salesman, and my brother had absolutely no interest in either of those things. He loved photography. But in my head, it still made sense to me that Dad was missing out by not having a son. I, on the other hand, loved nothing better than walking around a job site with my dad, playing architect and helping him sell homes.

My astronaut dreams had taken a back seat by then, but I learned a lot about running a business by following my dad everywhere. I also got to use a computer for the first time at his office, which introduced me to my life-long love of technology.

Following Dad around made me feel a little less alone, and I think he felt that way too. I know he missed Robert, but Dad and I formed a closer bond as I learned from him. I had always enjoyed hanging around his job sites while Robert was alive, but now Dad seemed to "see" me when I was there. I didn't realize it at the time, but I had made a vow to myself that I would achieve everything I thought my brother was going to achieve if he had lived. I did not have conscious realization about that vow until last year.

As I journeyed through my spiritual classroom, I explored Judaism, Buddhism, metaphysics, and meditation. I even read about ancient religions like the druids, Aztecs, and Mayans. The Indian, Egyptian, Greek, and Roman gods and their mythologies were eye-opening as they seemed to have many intersections.

I learned Reiki, did a few past-life regressions, went on a vision quest, prayed in some of the holiest places in the world, and experienced other places that just moved me with their beauty and silence.

Being raised Roman Catholic, I thought I should look at the other versions of Christianity—so I went to Protestant, Congregational, Lutheran, and Church of England services. I visited many churches, synagogues, mosques, and temples all over the world as I traveled. I found that every single one had a common thread and language that led them on the same search for why they were here and how they could achieve an eternal life with their God.

Books often created more questions for me—which made me read more books, visit more houses of worship, pray more, and speak to random strangers about their spiritual beliefs. I am still not at the end of my search for answers about God, but I have learned that God is within me even when I am angry at Him. I have felt and heard God in my life, and seen how His hand directs things even when it seems like I am in the midst of something bad for me at the time.

My brother always seemed to have such peace around him even when he was not feeling well. Reflecting back on my life, I realized that I had felt like my peace and safety disappeared when Robert died, and I seemed to lose the ability to relax. Some would say that my anger with God and disconnection from Him is what made me lose my peace and sense of safety and that connection with God was what gave Robert his.

I don't know about that, but I do know that as I have come to peace with what and who God is in my life, I smile more, handle stress better, and overall I am happier and more successful. I have learned to look beyond myself, expanding my awareness to a bigger picture that I fit into, and that helps me understand that I may not see the results of actions immediately. I know now that there are bigger results than I can see with my limited vision.

REALLY, ONE MORE THING?
CAN'T I EVER CATCH A BREAK?

The saying goes that God doesn't give you more than you can handle; and what does not break you will make you stronger. Did you ever feel like you wish God would just pay a little more attention to someone else, and give you a breather? I mean really, why does it seem like God pays more attention to some people than others?

In 2011, as I said earlier, both my mom and husband had to undergo heart surgery. Mom's surgery was eight months after my husband's, and the doctors and nurses all commented on how I knew the drill and was an old hand at the surgery and recovery process. I may have been an old hand on a clinical level, but on an emotional and faith level, I was a little shaky.

I mentioned in the last chapter how gathering with the prayer team at my church made me realize I was living in the fear mind versus the faith mind, and it was making it impossible to function. That awareness allowed me to fill my mind with faith that the outcome would be whatever was meant to be, versus the worst possible scenario.

I was walking my dog, Frankie, before I took Mom to the hospital for surgery. I was praying for God to fill my mind with thoughts of Him versus fear, when I heard the Cover Girl cosmetics commercial jingle. It was so loud in my head I actually looked for a source outside myself—which was unlikely to exist since it was four a.m. Sure enough, it was just Frankie and me, and the stars and trees outside.

I had heard a voice say, "No, I am just letting you know the surgery will be easy, breezy, and beautiful. All will be well today!" Then I felt this wonderful breeze blow through me, and my fears completely melted away.

I started crying and laughing and ran into the house to tell my mom. She said, "I already knew that."

When we got to the hospital, staff used the same words to me that I had heard in the breeze, "It will be easy, breezy, beautiful." I knew it was going to be okay because I had faith that Mom was in good hands. It was a different experience than I had felt at other points in my life, and I knew that I now had more conscious proof that there was something bigger than me.

Twice in my life I had personal experiences with what I believe to be guardian angels saving my life. I believe that personal faith in something bigger, with greater purpose than what we can understand, is what allows miracles to happen.

Asking myself,

- *Am I in fear?*

versus, allowing the fear to control me shifts me out of the dark and into a lightness of heart. A friend once said to me that when you feel that everything and everyone is against you, you just need to say,

- *Hey Jesus, Satan is knocking. Can you please answer the door?*

Now, I believe in Jesus and in evil—whether I call it Satan or the devil or just evil—so directing the question to Jesus works for me. It is just an example to show you that when I put my faith and belief in something bigger than me, the fear no longer keeps a locked hold on me.

Sounds kind of simple, doesn't it? Try saying it the next time you are in an argument (you may need to say it in your head and not out loud though), or when you are stuck in a sad place, or feeling like the world is against you. It really works for me to shift my thinking and allow in a peaceful presence to soothe me and begin moving me forward again.

IT'S NOT ABOUT THE BUILDING

It is not easy to talk about my faith and the path that got me to my beliefs today; but I feel it is important to show that I have a faith in spite of the difficult things I have gone through in my life. They actually brought me closer to God—but not to religion.

As a woman, the religion I grew up with had no real place for me—but the God I grew up with does. That, to me, is what matters in the end. Mine is a personal relationship and not an institutional one. My faith has an intellectual component to it. But when I ask myself,

- *Why do I believe?*

I realize the answer is just, "Because I do." I need to believe in a higher purpose and being because it helps me put one foot in front of the other each day.

That moment when I accepted my faith in God into my heart versus just believing it in my head was nothing I can ever explain on an intellectual level. That was difficult for me at first, since I have relied on scientific explanation and reasoning my whole life. The book, *The Shack*, by William Paul Young, really helped me relate to why God lets bad things happen to good people.

I had always had difficulty with the concept of God as three separate beings, but the idea that Jesus and the Holy Spirit are one and the same with God but just a different aspect of His personality made total sense to me. Some Christians may disagree with the way I phrase this, but it is what brought me to a deeper, more personal relationship with God.

I feel there are many ways to approach that moment when you accept God for who He is. Everyone learns differently and has to unlearn much of what has been programmed by man-made religions. At the end of the day, it is your individual relationship with God that determines your faith—not how often you go to church, how much you tithe, or how humble you are. Yes, all those things help us connect to God; but they are not what feeds the soul relationship with God.

My husband and I go to church on a regular basis because we learn more there than we would if we were just to recite words from memory. We go to a Bible-based church versus Catholic or Baptist (he was raised Baptist), because we feel connected there.

I loved my Catholic church in Connecticut (thanks Father Mike for inspiring me to get a deeper relationship with God), but the Catholic churches near us in Florida felt empty to us. We have a lot of friends who go to them on a regular basis; but for us, at the writing of this book, Calvary Chapel, Melbourne, is our faith family.

The community is what it is all about for us. Being amongst other people who believe as we do, for the most part, enables us to spend that time in church in a deeper connection with God. Our pastor also has wonderful insights into the Bible which helps us deepen our faith.

What I learned is to ask myself,

- *Why do I go to church or why don't I go to church?*

I found I wasn't going to church because it didn't mean anything to me. By exploring other religions, I learned what God meant to me and how to have a relationship with Him. I realized I did not have to follow a religion just because it is what my parents did. I needed to find my own spiritual path.

Faith is at the end of all spiritual journeys, and every religion I explored seemed to go back to one universal God. Why can't they all be the same God with different aspects of Him appearing to guide us to Him?

I am sure I will get a lot of email and mail from my views here, but I hope you will go away with an answer for yourself to the questions:

- *Do I believe in God?*
- *What does that mean for me?*

Questioning religion and faith is good. It means you care enough about the answers to explore what they mean for you. Just remember to be open to the answers you get. They may come from unusual and unexpected sources—like a breeze!

?????
Questions to Ask Along the Way

In regards to faith, ask yourself:
- Do I believe in God?
- Am I in fear?
- Hey Jesus, Satan is knocking. Can you please answer the door?
- Why do I believe?
- Why do I go to church or why don't I go to church?
- Do I believe in God and what does that mean for me?

Wise Woman Notes

WISE WOMAN NOTES

Chapter 10

What Would a Wise Woman Do? In Planning Her Future

"Never, ever give up your dreams…because even though they may seem far away, they could come true tomorrow."
—Rose Nyland, The Golden Girls

"You attract what you are, not what you want."
—Dr. Wayne Dyer

Do You Want the Dream?

I don't know about you, but I have always wanted to live the dream I had in my head of the perfect life: a life filled with princess moments and abundance. I felt like I had moments of my dream throughout my life, but I could never maintain the dream life. The other shoe always seemed to drop—taking with it the joy of the dream. One moment I would be on top of the world, and the next I would be struggling to make sense of something that put my dreams on the back burner. I might be impacted by health issues, family or business problems, or random events that affected the world around me—like 9/11 or the massive tsunamis.

WANT = LACK

I felt I should be able to hold my dream in spite of what was occurring around me; yet despite trying, and I mean I tried really hard, I couldn't. Then I met John David Mann, *NY Times* bestselling author and speaker, who told me that when you say, "I want," you are telling the universe that you lack something. BAM, it was like someone had hit me on the head with a two-by-four. I realized every time I said I wanted something, it focused me on the idea that I didn't already have it.

Think about your "want" statements. Do you say, "I want love, I want money, I want a better job, I want a bigger house, I want a new car?" Or do you say, "I have an incredible life filled with abundance and love and I have everything I need?"

With these new thoughts in my head, I started to go back through my past and look at the times of abundance and the times of lack. I tried to pinpoint my thoughts at each point in time. I realized I had more "want conversations" when I was in perceived lack than when I felt I was living my dreams.

So what did that mean for me? It meant that I needed to learn to choose my words carefully so more of my dream could be allowed in—versus using words that said I wasn't living my dreams.

It is not easy for me, or most women for that matter, to give ourselves permission to be happy, have our dreams, and focus on ourselves first. Dr. Wayne Dyer, in his movie, *The Shift*, quotes a study on the moment that turns your values upside down. In that study, women were researched over a period of many years and asked what drives them and what they need.

Once a shift had occurred in them, the response dramatically changed. They went from putting family and others first—to living their dreams and putting their own happiness first. Gretchen Rubin describes this shift so perfectly for me in *The Happiness Project*.

Rubin observed that the happier she became in her life, the more those around her became happy—which increased her happiness even more. It seems like the opposite of what we have been taught—but I encourage you to try it and see what happens around you when you become happier by putting yourself first.

Some people may drop out of your circle of friends (remember we talked about this in Chapter 4) because they don't want you to be happy. I have learned that there are people out there who revel in our unhappiness to the point of reinforcing it. If we hang out with them too much, eventually we cannot see anything else. That keeps us in victim mode—and you cannot be happy if you feel victimized.

Smile at random strangers, and watch how they shift. Be happier at your job, and see how much better you perform, and how your coworkers' energy changes. Basically, live your life as if you are already living your dream, and watch how your dreams begin to actualize around you. It is like you are attracting your dreams with a very strong magnet.

That is what Wayne Dyer's quote is all about for me. If you tell the world you want something, but don't act like you deserve it or already have it, you will never be able to hold it when you do receive it.

You have to act in order to fulfill your dreams though. You cannot just wish your future into existence. It takes work and dedication, and it will only happen if you are in alignment with who you truly are.

If you are not good at math, you will probably never become the next Albert Einstein, even if doing so is what you want. But you could study really hard and learn all you can about math to become a math professor or accountant. Would you be deeply happy? Probably not, and that is why it is important to understand who you are, and not who others want you or have led you to be.

I was interviewed for a job once, and they asked me why I had applied. The only answer I could give them was it seemed the next logical step in my career path. Do you think I got that job? No. Am I glad I didn't? YES! Not getting that job showed me I was making choices based on shoulda, woulda, coulda versus what made me light up from the inside out.

As a Wise Woman, you need to be asking yourself,

- *What lights me up about my day, my life, my job, my environment?*

Once you have an idea, search out more of those experiences and one day you will realize that you are living your dream. It just might not be the dream you originally envisioned for yourself! That is wonderful, because as we grow, our vision changes—just like our taste buds change from hating broccoli to loving it. (At least that is what happened in my case.)

Be open to what is in your life versus what you feel you want. You may see that the next time you say, "I want…" you immediately ask yourself,

- *Why do I want "xyz"?*

Then you can ask yourself:

- *How do I shift my thinking so that I can attract whatever I need in order to achieve my goal of …..? Maybe even world peace!*

LOVE YOURSELF ENOUGH TO ALLOW LOVE INTO YOUR LIFE IN EVERY FORM.

The core of all abundance and wisdom is love. *Love yourself enough to allow love into your life in every form.*

It doesn't matter what happened in the past in your life. What matters is what you do now—creating your next step, and your next, and your next. Only you can create the life you want in your future, and you have to begin living it openly.

If you want more love, be more loving. If you want more money, understand your relationship with money, and see how you can make a difference with what you have. If you want a better career, shift how you think about your current job, and pursue other interests until you find the career that lights you up.

Saying you want a better career or more money, yet not doing what it takes to earn more money or get that promotion, is just wishful thinking. Act as you wish to be treated. Live as you wish your life will be. That does not mean going into debt so people think you are prosperous though. Watch what begins to happen when you embrace and live the feelings you have as you see the "dream you" becoming the "real you."

I did a test once while conducting corporate training. I was going to be leaving on a trip right after work, so I had packed some vacation clothes to change into before I left for the airport. At the last moment, I decided to teach the class while wearing leggings and a beach shirt rather than my suit.

The reactions were amazing. The students, all adults, weren't as attentive to what I had to say. They talked amongst themselves more than in other classes I'd taught wearing a suit, took longer breaks, and rarely looked me in the eye. At the second break, I stopped them and asked them what their perception was of me that moment.

There was almost universal perception that I was very young, did not know what I was talking about, and was not of their intellectual group. That last assumption was interesting since I had more college degrees than the majority of the people in the room at the time.

Now, I worked with some of these people on a regular basis, and they had been taking the class for several days prior to my "clothing test." Since I was teaching them how to interact with and facilitate change in people with limited traditional education, I thought this test was important since the people they would be working with would not be dressed like them.

After challenging their perceptions with this test, I saw, as did they, how acting and dressing (or not acting and dressing) a part can often shift people's opinion of you. Think about the last time you saw a kid on the street with his pants hanging below his boxer shorts. What did you think about him? What about the guy wearing the khakis and a polo shirt?

Sounds pretty cliché right? Clichés exist for a reason; they are true for the most part. Your future is now—a much overused cliché— but it's true, because the moment you say, "I wish," you have already stepped into a future moment. So there is no better time to start creating your future than now.

Hopefully you have already written out your dream letters that I discussed throughout this book. But maybe you haven't because you are like me and like to finish a book before you dive into the changes that you feel shifting in you while reading. Don't worry if you haven't written anything down yet, because the beauty of change is it can start at any time. Your choice!

?????
QUESTIONS TO ASK ALONG THE WAY

In regards to your future, ask yourself:

- What lights me up about my day, my life, my job, my environment?
- Why do I want "xyz"?
- How do I shift my thinking so that I can attract whatever I need in order to achieve my goal of …?

WISE WOMAN NOTES

WISE WOMAN NOTES

WHAT WOULD A WISE WOMAN DO? TO GET STARTED

"To solve any problem, here are three questions to ask yourself: First, what can I do? Second, what can I read? And third, who can I ask?"
—Jim Rohn

"BUT WHERE DO I START?"
START EXACTLY WHERE YOU ARE!

I thought about ending with just that line, but I thought you might like a little more detail—as I would if I were you. The reason I say, "Start exactly where you are," is that too often we feel we have to be at a different point in the process before we can possibly hope to make any changes. To use another cliché, "a journey of one thousand miles begins with a single step," and you already took a first step. ***You read this book.***

Charles "Tremendous" Jones said, "You will be a different person five years from now based on two things: the people you meet and the books you read." Therefore, you are already a different person than you were when you started reading.

This book is not about a one-path process for getting yourself off autopilot. It is about getting you to think about your responses to life's answers before you accept them as the only answers. I say it is about the answers versus the questions because it is often easier to see that asking a different question would have served you better once you hear the answer to your initial question.

With practice, you will be able to anticipate what the answer may be to the questions you are asking before you ask them. That will give you the opportunity to change the question before you actually say it out loud. It is not a perfect science, but I use a quick reminder phrase before I do any of the following: start a new project, ask someone for help, take a new job, enter a relationship, make a purchase, have that extra piece of chocolate cake, or get angry. I ask myself (and you can ask yourself as well):

• *What would a Wise Woman do?*

Then I respond from that place. If you are a brave guy who read this book, feel free to use the same question or substitute, "What would a Wise Man do?"

If you are not happy with your relationships, business, career, health, life, or faith—or you just feel that there has to be something more—I encourage you to sit down and write a letter to a friend, God, or to me if you prefer, describing in wonderful detail what your life is like, *as if you are already living your dreams.* I have posted a copy of the letter I wrote so many years ago on www.WhatWouldAWiseWomanDo.com.

You are welcome to look at it if you need some inspiration to get started. Don't copy mine though, as it must be what comes from your soul. And last time I checked, we were all unique in how we reach our full potential!

Whether you are struggling or doing well, I urge you to consciously write down your version of you and your life without the baggage of your past, the opinions and programming of those around you, or your own ideas of who you should be. This will free you from autopilot and open new possibilities and pathways to an unlimited future.

Once you finish the letter, you can send it to me if you want—but really this letter is for you and the bigger you. Read it out loud to give real life to the intention in you and out there. The results may not be seen overnight—but then again, they might!

Now, put your hands on the steering wheel of your life, place your foot on the accelerator, turn off the autopilot, and turn into who you truly are: A Wise Woman!

Author's Note

Dear readers and fellow Wise Women: I wish for you a life filled with joy and love, dreams and fulfillment of those dreams. I pray that you find what you are seeking and are able to show others how they may find what they are seeking. There is no greater tool for learning than to show someone else how you have learned, changed, blossomed, and loved.

For more questions to ask yourself along the way, and a place where you can continue this journey with other Wise Women, go to <u>www. WhatWouldAWiseWomanDo.com</u>. When you create a free account, you will receive daily emails with questions to keep you off autopilot for the things that matter. As always, I promise to never sell your contact information. It is just so I can respond to you.

Once registered, you can also participate in forums where you can share ideas, struggles, questions, and more with others on the journey to become wise and you can even download free tools to guide you.

I thank you for taking this journey with me, and I am looking forward to hearing about how you have moved forward—and the questions you asked yourself to get there. Drop me a note on my website, or send me an email at

WiseWoman@WhatWouldAWiseWomanDo.com.

Now get busy asking some questions and remember, asking the *right* questions can change your life. So choose your questions wisely.

ACKNOWLEDGMENTS

Cool, you are actually reading this! I love to read author acknowledgments to see who they feel is worthy of mention—and sometimes to learn a little more about who inspires them. So onto it then!

You already know how I feel about my mom and dad; my husband, Jerome; and God; based on my dedication at the beginning of the book (you did read that, didn't you?)—so I will continue this with some other people that I am ever grateful for in my life.

For my publishers and mentors at Morgan James Publishing— David Hancock, Rick Frishman, and Scott Frishman—who heard me and believed in me when all I had was a concept for this book. I am blessed to have on my team my agent, Michael Ebeling, and my attorney Peter Hoppenfeld— who guided me along my new path as an author and did it with laughter and astute business sense.

For my mentors, Gary W. Goldstein, Peter Hoppenfeld and Rick Frishman of Mentoring365—thank you for demonstrating that being true to yourself leads to wonderful things. Yes, I know I mention some of these guys a few times but really, I am crazy grateful for them in my life!

For Brendon Burchard, who introduced me to my publisher, and through the publisher to my agent, and also opened my eyes to some areas I was still on autopilot. I know it sounds backwards, getting the publisher before the agent, but I rarely do anything in a specific way just because someone says I should do it in a certain order.

I am grateful for Jocelyn Godfrey of Spiritus Communications, my editor, who made my words better and asked me some great questions to enrich this book. I hope you think so too. For my author's team at Morgan James—including Lyza and Jim—for guiding me through the details of getting *What Would a Wise Woman Do?* from manuscript to finished book.

Thank you my dear friend David Riss of Greyskye Marketing for your advice on style and design. Your input was invaluable during the creative process.

Thank you Bob Burg, well, for being Bob Burg.

Father Mike Boccaccio—you reintroduced me to God so I could see Him differently, and as a result opened my heart to possibility again. I don't think there are words to express the magnitude of how my life changed because of that.

Pamela Adan, Cheri Abrams, and Gini Murphy—you got my physical body working again, which opened my mind to how I was stopping myself from moving forward; your friendship made it safe to do so.

This book might not have made it to the bookshelves on schedule without Jessica Pescha of Indian River Acupuncture—Jessica, you cleared my writer's block with N.E.T. and got me in the flow again. Who knew writer's block is really just an emotional block!

Thank you, Keith Alstedter of Deersong Transformations. You have guided me into the light of me for the last eighteen years with joy and tears but always with love. Thank you for seeing me even when I wasn't seeing myself.

Thanks to Sue Graves for your knowledge and friendship for close to half my life, it seems. You opened my mind and body to the world of homeopathy, and held me together while my body seemed to be failing. And sometimes you just held me when I needed a hug from a friend.

Thank you Susanna Isaacson for holding the faith for me as I began a closer walk with God and for introducing me to Jerome. Your prayers, friendship, and love have been an anchor for me over the past few years.

To my Aunt Theresa and Uncle Richard—thank you for always encouraging me and letting me hang out with you when I just wanted family around or needed a bit of opera!

I would be remiss if I didn't say how grateful I am for the best mastermind team God could have created for me. Alex Laws, Koya Noe, and Linda Stirling—my life is even more blessed and this book got finished because the three of you are in my life.

Thanks to Art Goetze and Mary Riesberg for your insights that got my book proposal accepted. And thanks to all those who read the various drafts of this book along the way: Roger Wernow, John Ertlmaier, Larry Baum, Gilda Ambrosino, Frank Mollica, Susanna Isaacson, Linda Stirling, Koya Noe, Randolph Kraus, and my incredible one-of-a kind mom. You are all the company I keep and I am truly thankful you are all in my life.

I am also deeply grateful for everyone on God's guest list for me. Your intersections in my life have created the woman I am today. Thanks to Debbie Macomber who first told me about creating God's Guest List.

Thank you, my readers—for whom I wish nothing but joy and possibility. Drop me a line at www.WhatWouldAWiseWomanDo.com and tell me what questions you are asking yourself, and let me know how you are moving off autopilot by asking questions.

INDEX
WHAT ARE THE QUESTIONS?

In regards to overall questions, ask yourself,

- What am I asking myself around "x"?
- Am I asking the best question(s) to move me forward and out of where I currently am?
- Do I know where I want to be?

In regards to where you are, ask yourself:

- Am I on autopilot?
- Am I responding from the Spock, Experience, or Reality Point?
- Am I ignoring signs I need to change direction?

In regards to questioning questions, ask yourself:

- What questions am I asking myself that got me to this place?
- Where did the questions come from?
- Do they still serve me?
- Are the answers I get moving the dial forward towards my goals, and does my questioning put me outside my comfort zone?

In regards to key questions, ask yourself:

- What would a Wise Woman do?
- What am I asking myself?
- How do I know if I am asking the right questions?
- How do I question my questions?

In regards to your circle, ask yourself:

- Who and what do I need around me to be a success?
- What in my life today is not helping me achieve my dream of being a successful business owner?

In regards to reality versus programming, ask yourself:

- Does the other person's reaction have anything to do with me and this situation, or is it about his or her history and fears?

In regards to finishing something, ask yourself:

- Why don't I want to finish this?
- What is stopping me from completing "xyz"?
- Will completing "xyz" move me towards my goals?
- Why did I start it?
- What are my expectations for what will happen when I finish…?

In regards to managing expectations, ask yourself:

- Was I clear and realistic with this person and with myself about what I wanted to receive?

In regards to having children, ask yourself:

- Do I want kids?
- Do I want them because I like being around them?
- Do I just want to have someone to take care of me when I get older?
- What does the warm feeling inside mean that I get when I hold babies?

In regards to asking why, ask yourself:

- Why am I doing this?
- Why do I want to do this?
- What can I do to change the outcome?
- Where can I get an answer?

In regards to pet ownership, ask yourself:

- Why do I want a pet?
- Am I prepared to make the time commitment involved with training, or am I better off getting an older pet that has already been trained?
- What kind of pet do I want—one I have to walk, or one that goes in a litter box or a cage?
- Am I willing to take on the responsibility for another being that relies on me completely for its entire lifespan?

In regards to friends, ask yourself:

- Do they challenge me to move forward or to stay where I am?
- Do they tell me the truth or the truth I want to hear?
- Are they successful at what they have chosen to do, or do they make excuses for why they fail?
- Am I the smartest person in my circle of friends?
- Do I dread getting emails or phone calls or running into these friends unexpectedly?
- How do I feel after I spend time with friend "x"?
- Are the friendships two-way relationships? This means, are they/ am I always taking or giving? If I am always taking, then it is time for me to ask myself why and stop doing that.

In regards to spouse or significant other, ask yourself:

- Why do I want to get married?
- Why am I doing what I am doing, and does it move me forward towards my goals I have for my future?
- Why do I have these goals? Are they mine or someone else's for me?

In regards to community or other commitments, ask yourself:

- Do I believe in my community?

- Why do they want me?
- What can I truly offer them?
- What impact can I make for them?
- What will doing/joining this mean for the other things I have on my plate?
- What do I get out of being involved?
- Does this relationship match my branding, or does it take me off track?

In regards to life or business, ask yourself:

- What can I do with my life that lights me up?
- What do I need to do to fully achieve that?

Chapter 5: What Would a Wise Woman Do? In Business................ 59

In regards to business overall, ask yourself:

- Am I happy right now, this moment, with what I am doing?
- What would make me happy?
- Why am I doing what I am doing?
- How will I feel after I make "x" decision?

In regards to staffing, ask yourself:

- Where do I want my business to be in one year, three years, five years?
- How do I want my life to look?
- What do I want people to be saying about the company?
- What does my ideal staff look like?
- Why do I feel I have to grow the company?
- Should I let him/her go?
- What type of person would be best suited for that position?
- Would it be better to shift someone from a position he or she is in to another position or hire a new employee?
- Can I outsource that position or use a search firm where I can try the person out as a contractor first?

In regards to partners, ask yourself:
- If it goes bad, what do you want the end result to be?
- Why do I believe I should add a partner?
- Does adding a partner move us forward more than I can without one?
- Do I need a partner or a strategic consultant instead?
- What do I want this partner to be doing?
- What will adding a partner do versus adding an employee?
- Do I really just need a cash infusion for growth?

In regards to clients and growth, ask yourself:
- Does the potential client fit our ideal client?
- Are we or they better served by passing the client along to another company better suited for their needs?
- Can I make money having this client?
- Am I ignoring any warning signs that this could be a problem client?

Chapter 6: What Would a Wise Woman do?
In regards to personal crisis, ask yourself:
- Can I take control of the situation?
- Is there one thing I can do right now that shifts the response I am getting, or makes the result a better one right now, this moment?
- What is wrong with me and what do I need to learn to heal myself?
- What can I do to change what is happening right now, this moment?
- What do I need to do to get through the next day?
- Who do I know or need to know that can help me?
- What questions do I need to ask myself and my doctors to get well?
- What do I need to change in my life that may be contributing to my health issues?
- Who can help me?
- Where and when do I feel best?

- In regards to family illness, ask yourself:
- What have I stopped doing because of what I think someone else will say or feel?
- Can I change it?
- May I speak with the charge nurse?
- What medications do you have my (*insert relationship here*) on and why?
- Is there anything I can do that will help you give better care to my....?
- How much experience do you have treating the illness you just diagnosed?
- What are the side effects to the medications, how long has the drug been used for treating the illness, and are there any alternatives?
- What will I be billed for and is there another option?

Chapter 7: What Would a Wise Woman Do?

In regards to a penny saved, ask yourself:

- What is it about that life that I want?
- Why do I want it?
- Is my striving for that (fill-in-the-blank) my need or someone else's?
- Why is this the way I define success?
- Where did that vision of success come from?
- Does this picture represent my belief about success, or is it someone else's that I adopted?
- Is there another way I can feel successful without all the material trappings?
- Does that belief serve me and my future?
- What are my financial goals?
- When I think about money, how does it make me feel?
- Have I written my list yet of what I want and/or need?
- Am I making long term or short term money choices?

In regards to self-perception, ask yourself:
- Will this piece of candy make me feel better in the long run or just the short run?

In regards to ANTS, ask yourself:
- Why am I letting fear rule me?

In regards to mind mirrors, ask yourself:
- Who am I being in my business or in my life—and is it really who I am?
- What do I believe about who I need to be in my business? My marriage? My family? My friendships? My community? My life?
- Do they reflect who I really am inside?
- Do I enjoy being that person?
- What would happen if I shed aspects of my personality that don't reflect who I am today?
- Is there anything I need to let go? Why?
- Do you just need me to listen, or do you want advice?
- Who is *my* best self?

In regards to faith, ask yourself:
- Do I believe in God?
- Am I in fear?
- Hey Jesus, Satan is knocking. Can you please answer the door?
- Why do I believe?
- Why do I go to church or why don't I go to church?
- Do I believe in God and what does that mean for me?

Chapter 10: What Would a Wise Woman Do?
In regards to your future, ask yourself:

- What lights me up about my day, my life, my job, my environment?
- Why do I want "xyz"?
- How do I shift my thinking so that I can attract whatever I need in order to achieve my goal of …?

WHAT DOES A WISE WOMAN READ?

I used a few quotes in the book that basically boil down to the idea that you are what you read. I love books of all kinds, and can easily read four books a month if my schedule permits. I am often asked what books I am reading, so I have decided to list a few of the books I have read that have influenced my life and moved me forward in my quest to have the best life possible.

I have also created a website, www.WiseWomenRead.com, to keep you up-to-date on my reading list. It includes my thoughts on each book as well. The website is more comprehensive than I have included here, and is ever-expanding, but you can subscribe to be notified when I post a new book. (Note: I will never sell your email address to anyone, and it will only be used to tell you about books I read.)

Feel free to send me the names of books that have impacted your life in a positive way, and perhaps they will make it onto the website! This list is in no specific order.

Steering by Starlight – Martha Beck
The Go-Giver – Bob Burg and John David Mann
It's Not About You – Bob Burg and John David Mann
The Happiness Project – Gretchen Rubin

Eat, Pray, Love – Elizabeth Gilbert

Living the Savvy Life – Melissa Tosetti and Kevin Gibbons

Life's Golden Ticket – Brendon Burchard

Positivity – Barbara Fredrickson

Change your Brain, Change Your Body – Dr. Daniel Amen

Guerilla Marketing – Jay Conrad Levinson

Thinkertoys – Michael Michalko

On Writing – Stephen King

The Maeve Binchy Writer's Club – Maeve Binchy

Stop Workplace Drama – Marlene Chism

One Month to Live – Kerry and Chris Shook

Traveling Light – Max Lucado

Atlas Shrugged – Ayn Rand

The Book of Awakening – Mark Nepo

Jesus Calling – Sarah Young

God's Guest List – Debbie Macomber

AND FOR FUN AND A FEW GOOD LIFE LESSONS AS WELL:

Dune – Frank Herbert

The Lord of the Rings – J.R.R. Tolkien

Harry Potter series– J.K. Rowling

ABOUT THE AUTHOR

 **Laura Atchison** is a speaker, author, and founder of Wisdom Learned, LLC—a consulting company specializing in educating and inspiring entrepreneurial leaders to get off autopilot and find success through lessons learned in the trenches.

Previously, Laura used her 29+ years' experience in both Fortune 100 and small businesses to launch and sell her own highly-competitive IT service company—garnering her recognition and coverage from national industry publications and associations as a leading provider of managed technology services.

Besides holding numerous technical degrees and serving on multiple charity and corporate boards, Laura holds a Master's degree in management. Her business and life philosophy gleaned from this diverse experience is simple: *Treat your customers, friends and family, better than they expect to be treated—while collecting and dispensing wit and wisdom to grow along the way. And **always** ask the right questions.*

Learn more or connect at LauraAtchison.com

CPSIA information can be obtained at www.ICGtesting.com
Printed in the USA
LVOW06s1751011113

359623LV00007B/796/P